Leaving Early
Undergraduate Non-completion in Higher Education

Mantz Yorke

UK   Falmer Press, 1 Gunpowder Square, London, EC4A 3DE
USA   Falmer Press, 325 Chestnut Street, 8th Floor, Phildadelphia,
PA 19106

First published in 1999

A catalogue record for this book is available from the British Library

ISBN 0 7507 0897 2   cased
ISBN 0 7507 0896 4   paper

**Library of Congress Cataloging-in-Publication Data are available on
request**

Jacket design by Caroline Archer

Typeset in 10/12pt Garamond by
Graphicraft Limited, Hong Kong

*Printed in Great Britain by Biddles Ltd., Guildford and King's Lynn on paper
which has a specified pH value on final paper manufacture of not less than
7.5 and is therefore 'acid free'.*

Contents

List of Figures and Tables

Figures

Tables

List of Figures and Tables

Acknowledgments

There are many people who have helped me, in one way or another, towards the writing of this book, and I give my thanks to the following.

- To Robin Bell, Alan Dove, Liz Haslam, Heather Hughes Jones, Bernard Longden, Catherine O'Connell, Rose Typuszak and Julie Ward (who all worked on the research with me) for their advice and support — and for making the work very much a team effort.

- To other colleagues in the project institutions who helped in various ways, by extracting data from records, assisting with their transformation into formats appropriate to the task in hand, and so on.

- To the students who completed questionnaires and responded to the telephone survey.

- To the students from Liverpool John Moores University who conducted the telephone survey and to Paul Cullinan for making the necessary arrangements.

- To Mick Youngman, Elaine Hodkinson and John Thompson for their advice on statistical matters.

- To the HEFCE for its sponsorship of, and to the Council's Steering Group for constructive comments regarding, the research on the 1994–95 withdrawers.

- To Anne Clarke, for invaluable secretarial work.

- To the following institutions which kindly provided information, on a confidential basis, from their own work on non-completion: Anglia Polytechnic University; the then Bath College of Higher Education; Bretton Hall College; Edge Hill University College; Homerton College, Cambridge; Imperial College; Keele University; King's College, London; Norwich School of Art and Design; Oxford Brookes University; Roehampton Institute, London; Sheffield Hallam University; Southampton Institute; UMIST; University College, Chester; University of Buckingham; University of Central Lancashire; University of Durham; University of Exeter; University of Kent at Canterbury; University of Luton; University of Salford; University of Sussex.

Acknowledgments

Some material in this book, particularly some of that in Chapters 6 and 7, originally appeared in Yorke et al. (1997).

Any errors of fact, interpretation or judgement in this book are my responsibility. The content of this book should not be interpreted as representing the views of HEFCE.

Mantz Yorke

List of Abbreviations

ACR   Average Annual Continuation Rate (used in the Linke Report from Australia)
AIR   Association for Institutional Research (United States)
AOU   Academic Organization Unit (Australia)
APL   Accreditation of Prior Learning
ASC   Academic Subject Category (used by HEFCE)
ASI   Approaches to Studying Inventory
AUCF   Average Unit of Council Funding (used by HEFCE)
BA   Bachelor of Arts degree
BTEC   Business and Technology Education Council
CERI   Centre for Educational Research and Innovation
EAIR   European Association for Institutional Research
ERIC   Educational Resources Information Center (United States)
FT   Full-time
GPA   Grade Point Average
HECS   Higher Education Contribution Scheme (Australia)
HEFCE   Higher Education Funding Council for England
HEQC   Higher Education Quality Council
HESA   Higher Education Statistics Agency
HESES   Higher Education Student Enrolment Survey
HNC   Higher National Certificate
IPEDS   Integrated Postsecondary Education Data System (United States)
IRR   Initial Retention Rate (used in the Linke Report from Australia)
IT   Information Technology
JPIWG   Joint Performance Indicators Working Group (United Kingdom)
LEA   Local Education Authority
MEng   Master of Engineering degree
OECD   Organization for Economic Cooperation and Development
PCR   Program Completion Rate (used in the Linke Report from Australia)
PT   Part-time
QAA   Quality Assurance Agency for Higher Education (United Kingdom)
SHEFC   Scottish Higher Education Funding Council
SPSS   Statistical Package for the Social Sciences
SW   Sandwich

Chapter 1

Non-completion: Important but Under-researched

Non-completion is political

Governments around the world are increasingly calling higher education to account for the money that is invested in institutions, as is evidenced by the rise of national quality assurance systems during the 1990s and the interest shown in performance indicators of various kinds.[1] The failure of undergraduate students to complete their studies is a cost to a government which funds higher education institutions and, *a fortiori*, is so where the government supports students through contributions to tuition fees and/or maintenance. A government's concern to keep public spending as low as possible means that the overt aspect of its economic agenda is best served by minimizing non-completion (or, to put it in more pejorative terms, by cutting 'waste').

However, the issue is not unidimensional. There is a general international perception that economies are best served by maximizing the level of education in the populace. In the United Kingdom, where participation was traditionally low (and non-completion was low), the government has presided over an increase in the participation rate at age 18 from about one in eight at the end of the 1970s to around one in three two decades later.

Correlating with this increase, the critical question for admission into higher education in the United Kingdom has changed over the years from 'Are you qualified to enter higher education?' to 'Are you likely to benefit from higher education?', with the latter (when answered in the affirmative) allowing many students into the sector who would otherwise have been excluded from it. Students from non-traditional academic backgrounds and from under-represented groups have been particularly encouraged to participate where some institutions have made a strong point of including 'access' in their missions. The corollary of widening participation is that the risk of non-completion is increased, placing one aspect of governmental policy (access) in tension with another (reducing public spending).

In other countries governmental policy towards higher education has been different, with relatively open access to the first year of full-time study being followed by much larger attrition rates (in Europe, notably Italy: see Moortgat, 1996; CERI, 1997). In Germany there has been concern for some years over a related issue, that of the extended period of time that some students have needed to gain their first degree.

1

Non-completion and delayed completion can be construed as ineffici-encies in the use of public finances, and hence they become political issues. In the 1994–95 academic year there were 764,359 full-time and 259,731 part-time students in English higher education institutions, who were enrolled on programmes up to and including the level of a first degree (HESA, 1996). The corresponding figures for the succeeding year were 789,139 and 341,482 (HESA, 1997). Information received from HESA indicated that in the 1994–95 academic year approximately 30,000 students discontinued, temporarily or permanently, their studies for one reason or another, but it is argued in Chapter 6 that this figure is about half of the true number.

Much attention was given during the mid-1990s to the increasingly diffi-cult financial position of students as the maintenance award was frozen (and hence suffered a decline in real terms), necessitating an increasing recourse to loans. The Committee of Vice Chancellors and Principals drew attention to the problem in press releases, and by 1996 the issue of non-completion had come to the fore as a matter of policy concern. There was, however, relatively little empirical evidence regarding the costs and causes of non-completion.

The developing political interest in non-completion can be seen in some of the media treatment of the release by the Higher Education Funding Council for England (HEFCE) of its report on non-completion in December 1997,[2] and of the publication in August 1998 of the *PUSH Guide to Which University 99* (Dennis, 1998). In the latter volume there is purported to be, for three-year programmes ending in 1996–97, an average 'flunk rate' of 19 per cent across institutions in the United Kingdom; this was rather extravagantly converted by Bentham (1998) into a cost to the taxpayer of some £360m.[3]

The empirical deficit

It is therefore surprising that student non-completion in higher education has been under-researched in Europe, Australia and New Zealand. Such literature as there is reveals a number of single-institution case studies but little that at-tempts to draw this information together synoptically. Differences in definitions and methodologies have made the robustness of findings problematic, and have made it difficult to coalesce findings from individual studies into a broader, synoptic picture of non-completion.

Amongst the few attempts to obtain a picture of non-completion from a broader perspective than that of a single institution in the UK are Johnes and Taylor's (1989, 1990a) analyses of completion rates in the then university sec-tor, Bourner et al.'s (1991) study of the part-time student's experience (includ-ing withdrawal), and McGivney's (1996) work on the experience of mature students in further and higher education. Using secondary data from five coun-tries in Europe, Moortgat (1996) conducted an analysis of non-completion, and in Australia McInnis et al. (1995) examined the first-year student experience in a number of institutions (it should be noted that the first year is of particular importance for withdrawal — in England about two-thirds of withdrawals are by first-year students).

The position is rather different in the United States, where institutional retention studies are routinely undertaken for the purposes of evaluation, policy formation and planning by offices of institutional research. Much of this work does appear in the public domain, if often only in the relatively unprestigious literature. However, with a few exceptions (e.g. Pascarella and Terenzini, 1991, whose brief was wider than retention and completion, and Tinto, 1993), there is relatively little that addresses the issue of non-completion from a synoptic perspective.

The theoretical deficit

Theory with respect to non-completion is underdeveloped, as is shown in Chapter 2. Tinto's (1993) model of departure has been the 'market leader' in research, and parts of the model have been tested by a number of researchers. There are a number of difficulties with this model (not least its level of generality), which make difficult the cumulation of findings from studies which have taken different slants. From the perspective of the researcher from the United Kingdom, the fact that finance is almost taken for granted by Tinto (because students in the United States have to determine prior to enrolment whether and how they can afford the costs of higher education) makes the model problematic for a higher education system in which, for some students, the enormity of debt only emerges as an issue after some time *in* an institution. In the United Kingdom students entering higher education since October 1998 have to pay, subject to means testing, a proportion of their tuition fees 'up front' and have to take out loans since the system of maintenance awards is being completely discontinued from the start of the academic year 1999.[4] This brings their position closer to that of students in the United States, and hence may give Tinto's model a better 'fit' with the system in the United Kingdom (though how long it will take for students to climb the learning curve of financial management in these new circumstances is a matter for conjecture at this stage).[5]

Tinto's work has also been criticized by those who approach non-completion from an interactionist perspective. A main plank of the criticism is that not enough attention is given to the perceptions of the students themselves, which are held to be of critical importance when the need to decide whether or not to continue comes to the fore.

Definitional problems

In the context of higher education in the United Kingdom (and no doubt elsewhere as well) non-completion is a slippery concept. From an institution's point of view, a student who transfers out to another institution is a 'non-completer' — yet the student may well progress to a degree without any loss of time: viewed from the perspective of the higher education system as a whole, it would be inappropriate to count such a student as a non-completer. Other students may take a period of time out of study (perhaps to have a baby, or to earn money to pay off a debt) and resume without having to retake any of their studies: in American parlance, such students would be described as 'stopouts' rather than as (pejoratively) 'dropouts'. Yet other students may need to retake a proportion of their studies, some with a period of intercalation. Although the evidence suggests that at present the numbers doing so are small, the future may see more students taking advantage of the flexibility inherent in credit accumulation schemes[6] by studying in mixed mode, in a distributed format and/or in more than one institution: how should such students be termed? The complexity of non-completion is compounded when account is taken of the difference between voluntary and involuntary non-completion, the latter being the case when the student does not do well enough to be allowed to progress to the next stage of the relevant programme of study.

In this book the institutional perspective has been taken, largely for pragmatic reasons and despite the inherent weaknesses. Students were thus recorded as 'non-completers' if they had disappeared from the student record system without having completed successfully the programme on which they had originally enrolled.[7] The research was based in institutions and used institutional databases as the source of information about the students who were recorded as having withdrawn. The returns from students indicated that institutional record systems were not always successful in identifying those who had transferred internally, and there were occasional instances where the institutional system had recorded the withdrawal of a student even though the student was continuing on the original programme. The proportion of responses of this sort was relatively small, but this does mean that figures from the institutional databases tend to give a slightly higher figure for non-completion (on the chosen definition) than is warranted. Work being conducted at sectoral level by HEFCE (but not yet published) is confirming the expected discrepancy between institutionally-based data and sectoral data.

It is obvious that the definition of students as 'non-completers' on this basis subsumes the 'stopouts' as well. The decision to study those who had left during, or at the end of, the two academic years 1994–95 and 1995–96 offered the opportunity to investigate the numbers of students who had transferred or who had 'stopped out'. The evidence presented in Chapter 4 shows that more than half of the full-time and sandwich[8] withdrawers had returned to study after a short period of time, though a substantial majority opted for a different institution the second time around. For part-time students, the proportion of returners was broadly similar, but those who had returned were more evenly divided between the original and another institution (this is not surprising, since part-time students tend to be limited to institutions within easy travelling distance from their homes).

Research questions

The general lack of knowledge in the United Kingdom regarding non-completion led HEFCE to commission two studies within the English higher education system:[9] a substantial quantitative study of those who had left during, or at the end of, the academic year 1994–95 conducted by a team led by the author (Yorke et al., 1997), and a smaller (largely qualitative) study conducted by a team from Keele University (Ozga and Sukhnandan, 1997). Yorke et al. were subsequently able to extend their work to include those who had left higher education prematurely in the succeeding year.

Three main questions underpinned the research, and are addressed in the chapters noted below. These chapters form the empirical heart of the book.

A.	What are the causes of non-completion?	Chapter 4 (full-time and sandwich students) and Chapter 5 (part-time students)
B.	How much does non-completion cost the taxpayer?	Chapter 6
C.	Could non-completion be used as a performance indicator and, if so, what would be the likely implications?	Chapter 7

Chapters 6 and 7 are largely self-contained in that they not only provide empirical findings but also draw conclusions from them.

The four empirical chapters are preceded by a survey of the literature (Chapter 2), which provides a broad picture of the state of knowledge of non-completion and related matters, and a brief description of the methods used to survey students' perceptions of the influences that bore on their non-completion (Chapter 3). Chapter 8 reflects on the outcomes of the surveys of the 'non-completers' and indicates where in the higher education system ameliorative action could be undertaken. The chapter concludes by revisiting Tinto's theorizing in the light of the evidence gathered as a result of the research.

Navigating the book

The book has been written with multiple audiences in mind, and hence sections will be of differential relevance to readers. Policy makers at national and institutional level will probably wish to concentrate on the concluding section of Chapter 2, the summaries at the ends of Chapters 4 and 5, and Chapter 8 (in which suggestions regarding action may be found), and to refer where necessary to the detailed evidence elsewhere in the book. Staff in subject departments and those responsible for student support services and quality assurance will probably find that they need to obtain the fuller picture of non-completion that is built up from Chapter 2 onwards. Appendices 4(a)(i) and (ii), in which comparisons on the basis of Academic Subject Category (ASC) for full-time and sandwich students can be found, should — with some diligence in scrutiny — raise a number of questions about possible differences between disciplinary cultures and practices, and about the quality of the student experience in multi-subject programmes.

It is likely that a book such as this will provide a point of reference for those researching the topic in their own institutions or more broadly in different national arenas. These readers will probably wish to concentrate more than most on the details of methodology given in Chapter 3. In a 'slippery' area such as non-completion methodology is not straightforward and compromises in data gathering and analysis have to be made.[10] Other researchers might wish to make different choices from those described in this book. In addition, researchers are more likely than most to wish to study the more detailed statistics that are provided in the appendices.

Notes

1. For a historical perspective on the development of performance indicators in the United Kingdom, see Cave et al. (1997).
2. This report subsumes Yorke et al. (1997) and Ozga and Sukhnandan (1997).
3. See Dennis (1998, pp. 13 and 791) for information about the 'flunk rate', and Clare (1997), Hodges (1997), Bentham (1998), Swain (1998) and Wojtas (1998), for example, for press comment on non-completion. In fact, the PUSH guide figures for 'flunk rate' are contested on the grounds that they do not represent the true situation fairly — for example, they count as flunking those students who merely transfer from three- to four-year programmes. Although the data on which the 'flunk rate' were obtained from the HESA individualized student record for the relevant years, HESA disclaims responsibility for any inferences or conclusions that might be drawn from them. Bentham's (1998) estimate of the cost of non-completion appears to be a 'worst case' figure, based on the assumption that all costs incurred by the state up to the moment when the student leaves are wasted expenditure: see Chapter 6 for an indication as to why, on the PUSH guide's 'flunk rate', this figure is about twice a reasonable estimate.
4. The academic year 1998–99 is a transition year in which the maintenance award is being phased out.
5. There are some similarities between the higher education systems of the United Kingdom and Australia insofar as tuition fee payment is concerned. In the latter country, students pay a proportion of their tuition fees according to the provisions of the Higher Education Contribution Scheme (HECS), but in their case repayment is income-contingent.
6. The flexibility does not extend to government provision of tuition fees, since fees for full-time and sandwich students are at least partially subvented whereas those for part-time students typically are not.
7. Some students may leave the institution with an intermediate award (such as a Certificate or Diploma in Higher Education) even though they were enrolled on a

first-degree programme. An unknown proportion may have originally intended to leave the institution at an intermediate stage but may have enrolled for the longer programme because they would then only have been required to pay a single enrolment fee rather than multiple fees for separate enrolments had they decided later to proceed to the first degree.

8. Sandwich students are those who have a period of work-related experience, usually of a year's duration, built into their programme of study.
9. Northern Ireland, Scotland and Wales have separately funded systems.
10. A fuller account of methods is given in Yorke et al. (1997b).

Chapter 2

What's Past is Prologue

Orientation

This chapter begins with theoretical approaches to non-completion in which the work of Tinto is prominent and shows that theory stands in need of further development. There then follow three sections devoted to empirical studies. The first of these is an overview of the vast literature from the United States, the second deals with the much more slender set of studies from the United Kingdom and the third reports a number of studies from other parts of the world. The final section extracts from this disparate literature a number of general conclusions regarding the causes of non-completion.

Theory

Theory relating to non-completion has been developed to the greatest extent in the United States where, for various reasons relating to institutional accreditation and funding, retention and withdrawal has been of considerable importance.

Astin (1991) implicitly offers a basic approach to withdrawal in his Inputs–Environment–Outputs (I–E–O) model in which inputs have a direct impact on outcomes as well as an indirect impact through various environmental factors. The I–E–O model is clearly very general and needs to be developed in detail with reference to whatever empirical investigation is being undertaken. One interesting implementation of the I–E–O model was undertaken by Kelly (1996) who had the advantage of a closed — and for that reason controlled — academic community of students in the United States Coast Guard Academy. Kelly was able to offer confirmation of the I–E–O model and, although he provides rather limited data in his report, some evidence to support the importance of integration, both academic and social, which features strongly in Tinto's (1993) more detailed theorizing.

From the point of view of student withdrawal, the I–E–O model can be elaborated in terms of student involvement. In his book *Achieving Educational Excellence* Astin (1985, p. 133) described his 'theory of involvement'[1] in simple terms: 'Students learn by becoming involved.' Astin offers five postulates:

- involvement requires the investment of energy (psychological and physical);
- students invest varying amounts of energy in the tasks facing them;
- involvement has both qualitative and quantitative features;
- the amount of learning is proportional to the quality and quantity of involvement; and
- the educational effectiveness of a policy or practice depends on its capacity to stimulate involvement.

What Astin does here is to focus attention on the commitment of the student and on the capacity of the educational environment to convert that commitment into valued outcomes. In so doing, he leads into the work of other theorists who have sought more explicitly to address the issues of persistence and non-completion.

The greatest influence on retention studies has probably been Tinto (1993), whose theory of student departure has been in the public domain for more than two decades. The notion of *integration*[2] is central to Tinto's theorizing: a student enters higher education with a set of background characteristics, intentions and expectations, and his or her decision to persist or depart is a function of the extent to which he or she has succeeded in becoming integrated into the institution socially and academically. Tinto suggests that, where the experience of the institution is negative, the individual tends to experience diminished academic and/or social integration and may come to the conclusion that the costs (academic, social, emotional and/or financial) of persisting outweigh the benefits of persisting. At that point, the individual withdraws.

Figure 2.1 A simplified form of Tinto's model of institutional departure (after Tinto, 1993, p. 114)

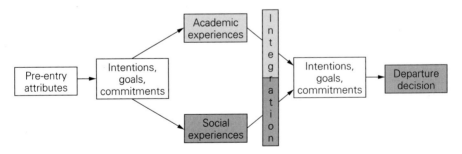

Tinto's model of institutional departure is given, in simplified form, in Figure 2.1. Tinto's theory appears rather self-contained in that it has relatively little to say about the impact of external factors in shaping students' perceptions, commitments and reactions; as a result, Napoli and Wortman (1997) have elaborated Tinto's model to acknowledge the impact of external factors. External factors may be of policy-related significance. In the American context, there are programmes which seek to encourage enrolment and to reduce attrition — for example, through special funding initiatives (see, *inter alia,* Folger and Jones, 1993). In the United Kingdom there is continuing concern at the relatively low participation from the working class (a matter which has been the subject of review by Robertson and Hillman, 1997) and government policy may be developed to address this issue — thereby influencing the context within which Tinto's modelling might be applied.

A second matter of contention with Tinto's approach is its lack of emphasis on the institutional contribution to withdrawal, since its general tenor is that of the student applying the calculus of advantage, rationally or otherwise, to the continuance of his or her studies. To be sure, Tinto's model can be invested with a perspective centred on the institutional contribution (since integration is bi- rather than unidirectional), but institutional failures, such as not making clear what the nature of a programme is or not providing a learning environment of an acceptable quality, seem to lie very much in the background. If non-completion is seen in wholly student-centred terms then there is some risk of blaming the victims of circumstances which are not of their own doing and of institutions failing to submit themselves to a level of self-scrutiny appropriate to the quality assurance activity that is expected of them.

Bean and various co-workers have, over the years, developed and tested a different model of attrition whose central proposition is that withdrawal is analogous to turnover in work organizations (see, *inter alia,* Bean, 1983, and Bean and Metzner, 1985). In Bean's model a student's beliefs (which are influenced by interaction with the institution and other students) shape attitudes which in turn shape behaviour. The model also acknowledges that extra-institutional factors can have an impact on individuals' decisions and, in this respect, appears stronger than Tinto's. The model was given some minor modifications by Metzner and Bean (1987) in order to deal specifically with attrition amongst part-time students. It was tested on 624 part-time first-year commuting students, and the authors commented favourably on the fact that 29 per cent of the variance was explained by the model. (This seems to be rather a low figure on which to base enthusiasm, but Metzner and Bean claim that it is nevertheless higher than in previous studies.) Metzner and Bean found that the main determinants of dropout were low grade point average (GPA), lower number of hours enrolled, lower satisfaction with the role of student, relative youth and a relatively restricted opportunity to transfer. Metzner and Bean concluded that their findings demonstrated the inappropriateness for part-time students of Tinto's model (because of its stress on social integration); they also expressed the view that the attrition of these students was most likely to be due to poor academic integration, which in turn was characterized by inferior academic ability or performance and a low level of commitment to study.

Although the literature tends to represent the Tinto and Bean models as alternatives, they do have a number of features in common — for example, they both acknowledge that students' background characteristics influence adjustment to the institution, that the persistence/withdrawal decision is dependent on a complex set of interactions over time and that the match between individual and institution is of importance (Cabrera et al., 1992). Indeed, Cabrera et al. sought to test, in an empirical study in a large urban commuter institution, the extent of convergence between the Tinto and Bean theories. They concluded (perhaps unsurprisingly) that the theories were complementary despite areas of overlap.[3]

Set against Tinto's and Bean's models relating to withdrawal, others have concentrated on the opposite side of the coin — that of student development. Here brief mention needs to be made of Pascarella's (1985) model of the determinants of change and Weidman's (1989) model of socialization. These are of peripheral importance to the present study, but both can be seen as 'insets' into the models of withdrawal in that, if learning and/or socialization are successful, then the likelihood of withdrawal is reduced.

Johnson and Buck (1995), responding to a Commission of Inquiry on Canadian University Education which claimed that 42 per cent of full-time undergraduates entering university in 1985 had failed to graduate within five years, constructed a model of withdrawal based on findings from 498 students in a Canadian university. The model, whose components will be familiar to those acquainted with Tinto's work, has students' academic and personal characteristics mediated by institutional factors to produce psychological states[4] and performances. Psychological state is associated with student decision-making regarding persistence and withdrawal, whereas academic performance is subject to institutional decision regarding continuation. In essence, the model makes the distinction between voluntary and involuntary withdrawal.

The most recent contribution to theory has been made by Ozga and Sukhnandan (1998), on the basis of responses from 41 withdrawers from a campus-based university in the United Kingdom. Ozga and Sukhnandan stress the importance of both preparedness for (full-time) university life and the compatibility of the choice that the student has made, and model these in a flow chart. Their model can be presented, in slightly simplified form, as in Figure 2.2.

Figure 2.2   Model of undergraduate non-completion (after Ozga and Sukhnandan, 1998). The uppermost chain is seen by Ozga and Sukhnandan as typical of mature non-completers

Preparedness for university life	Compatibility of institutional and course choice	Cause of withdrawal	Outcome
High	High	Unplanned external crises	Return home
Low	Low	Recognition of incompatible choice(s)	Go to new institution
Very low		Unpreparedness	Go into employment

Ozga and Sukhnandan's model appears to make the causality of non-completion less complex than it actually is. Compatibility of choice, for example, subsumes a number of variables such as the geographical environment, the institution, the academic organizational unit, the study programme as a whole and possibly components of the study programme. Incompatibility in respect of any or all of these can be causal in non-completion, as evidence presented later in this book suggests. That some students enter employment after withdrawal is to be expected; the issue which the model does not address is the likelihood of their returning to higher education. Evidence presented later suggests that other variables not in the model, such as social class, may be of importance here.

It is clear from this discussion that theory relating to non-completion stands in need of further development. Many of the terms that are used are portmanteaux and able to be interpreted in various ways. This perhaps reflects a failing on the part of theoreticians to address the needs of different audiences. For national policy purposes, a 'broad sweep' is probably all that is needed, since local institutional and individual circumstances are of relatively little account. Institutions, on the other hand, are likely to need a more fine-grained perspective on non-completion as they seek (for various reasons) to minimize it.

Given the complexity of the influences on withdrawal, it is preferable to view non-completion in terms of interactions (mainly between student and institution) rather than in terms of the pathology of the student. The interactionist view sees the student's perceptions and interpretations of reality as central, and hence the primary research need is to ask students what these are. The retrospective survey whose findings are presented later in this book is one way of approaching the problem at a relatively 'mass' level; smaller qualitative (and also retrospective) studies such as that used by Ozga and Sukhnandan (1997) allow individual students' perceptions to be studied in greater detail. What is missing is substantial longitudinal evidence which would enable the various models that have been put forward to be refined with reference to their underlying dynamics. There is still too little understanding in the United Kingdom of how potential influences on non-completion actually precipitate it; without this, it is difficult to see how theory might be taken forward in any substantial way.

Empirical findings

There are two main problems with the empirical findings relating to non-completion: much of what has been found in the United Kingdom relates to circumstances which were quite different from those of the present national context, and much of what has been found in other countries suffers some attenuation in usefulness because of cross-cultural differences. Further, much of the research into retention and non-completion has been undertaken at the level of the single institution and therefore has limited generalizability. This may have stimulated the exchange of views between Johnes and Taylor on the one hand, and McPherson and Paterson on the other, regarding the relative virtues of collecting data at the institutional level and the individual level, respectively (see, in sequence, Johnes and Taylor (1989), McPherson and Paterson (1990) and Johnes and Taylor (1990b)). The simple observation on this debate is that both approaches have their uses — which is to be used depends on the focus of the investigation. Institutional data have particular relevance for econometric modelling at the level of the system, whereas individual data are particularly helpful to institutions as they grapple with the challenge of understanding and minimizing non-completion.

Some studies from the United States

As one might expect, given the extensive and long-standing interest in the United States, there is a plethora of institution-specific studies in the literature. Institutions in the United States typically have offices of institutional research whose brief includes the collection of data relating to retention and their interpretation for institutional policy purposes. Much of this work finds its way into the public domain through presentations at Forums of the Association for Institutional Research (AIR).[5] Less attention has been given to the cumulation of findings, perhaps because the data from the individual studies are not easily brought together.

Pascarella and Terenzini (1991) undertook an extensive review of the way that higher education institutions affected students and, although their work did not specifically focus on non-completion, it is possible to find a number of general conclusions from their analysis of the vast body of research which relates to non-completion. There seems no reason, to judge from a number of institutional studies that have been presented at recent AIR Forums, to indicate that matters have changed appreciably in the intervening years. The following conclusions, *inter multa alia*, were drawn by Pascarella and Terenzini.

- Institutional quality and, in particular, selectivity significantly enhance institutional persistence and educational attainment (p. 375). However, enrolment in prestigious institutions is of high cost in terms of finance and educational effort, and there is an obvious disincentive against leaving without graduating. Institutional selectivity, however, has a negative indirect influence on outcomes when students' entering characteristics are taken into account, leaving the overall effect of institutional quality on educational aspiration and attainment as 'modest' (p. 376).[6] (A number of influences would seem to be impacting here, and it may be that stratification of institutions would allow the contributions of potentially antagonistic variables to be unscrambled.)
- The type of institution is likely to exert an effect. A 'commuter institution' is less likely than a residential institution to have a social system facilitative of social integration (p. 414).

- A high degree of uncertainty about a student's choice of academic major tends to be positively related to withdrawal (p. 426).
- Scholarships and grants tend to have the greatest beneficial effects on persistence (pp. 406–7).
- Social involvement is important in enhancing the persistence of students who have low levels of institutional and goal commitment (p. 412). As the level of institutional and goal commitment increases, so social involvement plays a decreasing role in persistence or withdrawal behaviour.
- Conversely, a high level of academic integration might compensate for a low level of social integration (p. 420).
- Campus integration, and consequently first-year persistence, are affected by a group of factors which include the extent to which the student is in employment (pp. 407–8). Full-time, and 'off-campus' part-time, employment are detrimental to campus integration, but part-time employment on campus has a positive effect on retention and completion.
- There is insufficient research on 'older, nontraditional students' (in United Kingdom parlance 'mature students') who, by 1986, constituted well over 30 per cent of all higher education students in the United States. There were no grounds for concluding that the factors influencing the educational attainment of 'traditional' students aged between 18 and 22 (typically in residential settings) applied to those who were older and who may have carried a greater number of responsibilities (p. 414).

The importance of expectations, stressed by Tinto (1993) in his model, was demonstrated by Braxton et al. (1995) who, in a survey of 263 first-year students in baccalaureate institutions, found that the meeting of students' expectations was positively associated with academic and social integration. This finding emphasizes the significance of positive 'feedback loops' in the student experience.

There is little in these findings that is counter-intuitive, although the differences between the United States and the United Kingdom in the way in which students are funded to participate in higher education may have an influence on persistence that cannot be identified from a study based on a single nation.

Seymour and Hewitt (1997), in a lengthy report that cannot be afforded justice here, studied the reasons why students departed prematurely from Science, Mathematics and Engineering programmes in the United States. Having established that some 44 per cent of students studying these programmes in four-year institutions 'switched' to other majors,[7] they undertook an ethnographic study of 460 students from 13 different institutions. In the light of the extensive qualitative data that they collected, they suggested that problems which arose from the structure of the students' educational experience and the culture of the disciplines (as reflected in the attitudes and practices of academic staff) contributed much more to attrition than did the inadequacies of the individual students or the appeal of other subject areas. Had the educational atmosphere been less 'cut-throat' and had staff been more supportive in personal terms, many who had left might have completed their original programmes satisfactorily; the authors noted that many female and non-white students appeared to fall into this category of potential completers. Seymour and Hewitt conclude that reform of the student experience would be needed if the 'drain' from Science, Mathematics and Engineering were to be reversed; while academics might relate this to curricular content and structure, of critical importance would be a stronger orientation towards the encouragement of student learning. The latter would have considerable implications for the way that staff interpreted their role as teachers. This study may well be of some significance to United Kingdom practice since non-completion rates in ASCs 4 and 6 (Engineering and Technology, and Mathematical Sciences, IT and Computing, respectively) are higher than the average for the sector as a whole.

In the middle ground between studies of retention and non-completion lies the issue of extension of the normal time to achieve a degree. Volkwein and Lorang (1996) looked at two behaviours adopted by full-time undergraduate students which they termed 'lingering' — extending the time taken to graduate and registering for less than the full diet of credits. The first has cost and efficiency implications for a number of stakeholders and the second bears on the efficiency of enrolment management. Volkwein and Lorang's multivariate analysis suggested that there were two main reasons for 'lingering': the desire to enjoy college life while at the same time protecting a high GPA, and the need for students to give themselves time to cope with work and family responsibilities (one notes here the attenuation of the term 'full-time'). The analysis also showed the importance to a student of having a financial need of sufficient magnitude in order to qualify for grant support. A number of variables relevant to Tinto's (1993) model were unrelated to 'lingering', implying that the lingering students were not significantly different from their peers who graduated in four years. Volkwein and Lorang's work sets down a marker for considering the implications of flexibility in participation under credit accumulation (and perhaps transfer) in the United Kingdom.

For some years now, Astin and various co-workers have been conducting research into higher education at the level of the system. Astin et al. (1996) examined the effect of a number of background variables on degree attainment rates; the emphasis was on completion rather than non-completion, but the use of a 'cut-off date' of up to nine years after enrolment on a bachelor's degree shows that the likelihood of many further graduations is rather small. In other words, those who have not completed in nine years (roughly half as long again as the criterion time reported by Gaither et al., 1995, as a performance indicator of completion[8]) are unlikely to complete. Table 2.1 summarizes the findings from a national sample of students from 365 baccalaureate-granting institutions who were freshmen in the 1985–86 academic year.[9]

Table 2.1   Cumulative graduation rates for a sample of 1985 entrants to higher education in the United States

	Per cent completing bachelor's degree within		
Unweighted n	*4 years*	*6 years*	*9 years*
79,814	39.9	44.9	45.7

Source: Astin et al. (1996, p. 4).

The percentage completion at nine years varied between 72.0 (private university) and 38.4 (public college), which is consistent with Pascarella and Terenzini's (1991) finding about completion in prestigious institutions, noted above.

Of interest also, as they provide markers against which data from the United Kingdom can be compared, are the differing completion rates of men and women, with the latter running at five percentage points above the former,[10] the differentials between racial groups and the fact that average high school grade[11] and Scholastic Aptitude Test score correlated positively with the nine-year completion rate.

Astin et al. discuss the use of regression analysis to produce expected attainment rates that can be set against the actually observed rates, and argue that if an institution has a good retention programme its actual rate should exceed its expected rate, with the opposite being true for a poor retention programme. Other 'environmental' variables, such as major field of study, selectivity of institution and residency during the freshman year, also have an impact on attainment rate and appear in the regression equation. The regression approach is attractive in theory but, in the United Kingdom system, there would at minimum have to be a valid and reliable method of assigning institutions to groups of cognate institutions if within-group comparisons were to be meaningful.

Studies from the United Kingdom

Research findings from the United Kingdom are, as was noted at the beginning of this chapter, institutionally based, related to an earlier ordering of the system or both. In addition, there has been inconsistency in both the methods adopted by researchers and — perhaps as a result — in some of their findings. From the perspective of contemporary higher education it is probably most helpful to group the empirical evidence under a set of general headings similar to those put forward by Woodley et al. (1987, pp. 159–60), which were:

- course factors;
- institutional factors;
- study environment factors;
- personal blame; and
- motivational factors.

Course-related factors

Thomas et al. (1996) reported that, for the academic year 1992–93, just over half of the withdrawing students cited course-related reasons as influences on their decision, though these were not disaggregated statistically. This finding is similar to that of Percy-Smith and Stronach (1992) who had earlier reported that the main reason for withdrawal was the unsuitability of the course, and that of Oakey and Rae (1994) who found 21 per cent of responding withdrawers indicating that the course had failed to live up to their expectations. More recently, Ozga and Sukhnandan (1997) found that the compatibility of the student with the choice of institution and/or course was influential in the non-completion of the majority of their sample of 'non-completers' at 'Campus University'.

To some extent these studies may reflect the influence of 'Clearing', where students who do not gain the grades needed to take up conditional acceptances from institutions have to 'shop around' rapidly during August and September in order to secure an alternative place in higher education. Moore (1995) noted that Clearing was the only route through which some students could gain entry to higher education, and Haslam and Chaudhry (1995) suggested that Clearing could be playing a causative role in withdrawal. There is a general view in the higher education system that, when students have to make rushed decisions about entry, this is detrimental to the 'goodness of fit' between student and institution and hence likely to increase the rate of withdrawal. As Haslam and Chaudhry put it: '. . . the picture here is one of mainly young people who discover that they have made a mistake, and withdraw to give themselves an opportunity to make a fresh start in adult life' (p. 5).

In a small-scale study of withdrawal, Rickinson and Rutherford (1996) found a group of students who felt that they would have benefited from a clearer understanding of the level and requirements of their course prior to enrolment. The students felt that their educational experience before entering higher education had not prepared them to cope with the rigours of degree-level study. Another group found difficulty in integrating socially. Although recognizing the limitations of their study, Rickinson and Rutherford concluded that their work supported the hypothesis that academic and social adjustment is the major influence on persistence and withdrawal.

The quality of teaching, and course content and level (within a broader category of frustrated expectations of higher education), were found by Moore (1995) to be the more often cited influences on withdrawal. In a study of students from further education Davies (1997) reported that withdrawn students had a significantly lower opinion of various aspects of the quality of the student experience than did students who had remained in college. These findings contrast markedly with those of Percy-Smith and Stronach (1992), in which teaching was barely mentioned as an influence, even allowing for the likelihood that these researchers' 'Course not suitable' category subsumed some aspects of course content and level.

Moore also found that a high proportion of withdrawers had been study-ing at off-site franchised courses, which, as McGivney (1996) points out, reflects the concern of writers such as Abramson (1994), Brady and Metcalfe (1994) and Bird et al. (1993) that these may fail to deliver the full richness of a higher education experience.

Institutional factors

Institutional — as opposed to programme — provision is relatively infrequently cited as a cause of withdrawal, perhaps because it is unlikely to be a precipit-ating factor. For example, only 1.4 per cent of the respondents in Percy-Smith and Stronach's (1992) study cited inadequate teaching/learning facilities as the single most important reason for withdrawing. However, institutional factors should not be too lightly disregarded, since a discrepancy between the student's expectations of an institution and the reality could contribute to dis-satisfaction and hence to the decision to withdraw. The increase in the numbers seeking entry to higher education since 1979 has led to intending students having less opportunity to gain a full appreciation of the institution and the potential programme of study than was the case in earlier years, as individual interviews have been replaced by open days and paper-based selection has grown. At the same time, prospectuses have sought increasingly to present institutions in a favourable light (how many rainy scenes or crammed lecture theatres are shown, for instance?), leading to some increase in the risk that students will be disappointed with the reality into which they ultimately arrive.

Johnes and Taylor (1990a) analysed non-completion rates for the then United Kingdom university sector. They used non-completion (rather than the attainment rate used by Astin et al., 1996) as the dependent variable and found that an equation combining A-level points score, residence in hall, whether the university was Scottish or not and whether or not the student was reading business, languages or social science could predict with only moderate accur-acy the actual non-completion rate. Johnes and Taylor suggested that, as there was a persistent pattern of non-completion across the then university sector, other institutional variables — such as the student gender ratio — might be having an influence on non-completion. Of importance to those who seek a simple indicator of performance relating to non-completion is their conclusion that '. . . the actual non-completion rate is unlikely to provide useful informa-tion about a university's performance' (p. 99). The greater complexity and diversity of the whole United Kingdom higher education system in the 1990s probably strengthen this message.

Extra-institutional factors

Woodley et al.'s term 'study environment factors' gives a misleading colouring to what are, in essence, matters in the student's life beyond the institution but which impact on his or her performance in it.

Of increasing concern has been the issue of students' financial circumstances, with the freezing (and, from 1998, the phasing out) of student maintenance grants, the introduction of loans and a tendency for programmes to
require students to fund 'extras' that in earlier times came as part of the institutional provision.[12] A substantial proportion of the respondents to Thomas et al.'s
(1996) survey specifically mentioned the cost of living as an influence on
their withdrawal. Recent studies reporting a significant impact of financial difficulty on withdrawal include those listed in Table 2.2 but, in contrast to these,
Oakey and Rae (1994) found that only 7 per cent of withdrawers cited financial difficulties, and Fennell (1997) found that only 1.9 per cent of respondents
to a survey of early leavers from the academic year 1995–96 cited financial
difficulties as the sole reason for non-completion, though the data which she
provides indicate that 19 per cent mentioned these as a reason.

*Table 2.2   Some studies which mention financial difficulty as a significant influence
on withdrawal*

Study	General topic of investigation
Thomas et al. (1996)	Withdrawal from an unnamed higher education institution in 1992–93
Percy-Smith and Stronach (1992)	Withdrawal from courses at Leeds Polytechnic
Foong et al. (1994)	The accelerated programmes piloted by HEFCE
Haslam and Chaudhry (1995)	Withdrawal from Liverpool John Moores University
Moore (1995)	Retention at Sheffield Hallam University
NUS (1995)	Student finances
Fennell (1997)	Exit and retention at the University of Derby
Johnston (1997)	Staff perceptions of first-year students' non-progression at a Scottish post-1992 university
Johnston (n.d.)	Withdrawal by first-year undergraduates at the same university

The NUS (1995) study of a sample of full-time students from two universities showed that student indebtedness had increased for each of three age
groups of students. Half of the respondents stated that their financial situation
was having an adverse effect upon their academic work; also cited as being
adversely affected by their financial position were health and the ability to buy
food and medicines. About one-third of the respondents had been employed
part-time during term, of whom two-thirds thought that employment had had
an adverse effect on their studies. Moore (1995), however, is at pains to point
out that financial considerations may nevertheless be secondary to a student's
decision to withdraw from study.

Staff and student perceptions may differ regarding the salience of financial
problems, judging by evidence from a Scottish post-1992 university. A survey
of staff perceptions undertaken in early 1996 regarding student withdrawals
during the 1994–95 academic year showed that 12 per cent of students were
thought to have left for reasons which included financial problems (Johnston,
1997). However, 25 per cent of students withdrawing from the same institution

two years later indicated that financial difficulties contributed to their decision to leave (Johnston, n.d.). It is probable that staff are less aware of students' personal difficulties than of problems relating to academic work and hence their perceptions will tend to be skewed.[13]

Percy-Smith and Stronach (1992) found that pressure of paid work and domestic commitments/problems were the second and third most frequently cited single reasons for withdrawal. Unfortunately, there is no indication in the report whether the students were full-time or part-time, so it is difficult to pursue their findings further. However, these findings echo others relating to part-time study (e.g. Bourner et al., 1991; Haslam and Chaudhry, 1995) where the pressures of the world beyond the institution are well recognized. Given the increasing pressure on student finances, it seems reasonable to give some consideration to the demands of employment on full-time study: Percy-Smith and Stronach's study may have been ahead of the game in 1992.

Thomas et al. (1996) found personal reasons to be cited by 60 per cent of the respondents to their 1992–93 institutional survey. It is clear that this category subsumes a variety of reasons from an inability to handle the totality of the higher education experience to the demands of home circumstances. Haslam and Chaudhry (1995) obtained a finer-grained set of responses from a sample of full-time and part-time students who withdrew from Liverpool John Moores University. The main reasons cited by the full-time students were family commitments (30 per cent), homesickness (23 per cent) and medical reasons (20 per cent). For the part-time students 47 per cent cited family commitments and 23 per cent medical advice.

Other factors impact unpredictably on withdrawal, such as illness and accommodation problems (Moore, 1995). Little is known about the extent to which students feel comfortable in the city or town in which they are studying. One example that surfaced as the HEFCE-funded project got under way was the impact of criminal activity (burglary and general harassment) on students in a particular area of Manchester which was reported in the local press (Holden and Ladbrook, 1995). This kind of problem has probably been replicated in other urban areas. With fear of crime at a higher level than actual crime levels, it is not unreasonable to suppose that location of residence may have some indirect impact on students' willingness to continue their studies.

Student background variables

Johnes (1990) analysed data from a sample of 328 students who entered Lancaster University in 1979 and found that students with high A-level results were less likely to withdraw or fail. This finding was supported by Johnes and Taylor's (1990) much larger study of national data for students entering the then universities at around the same time. Richardson (1995) found that, for his sample of mature students, there was a similar positive relationship between A-level points and degree class. These findings have to be set against a literature which tends to show low, but positive, correlations between A-level qualifications and degree performance (with the exception of mathematics and science-based studies, where the correlation is typically rather higher) — and also the experience of the former polytechnics and colleges sector, where a wider range of entry qualifications is the norm and where there is evidence that students entering without A-levels can perform as well as their A-level entrant peers (see, for example, Wrightson, 1996).

Johnes and Taylor (1990) also found that, for cohorts entering United Kingdom universities over the period 1975–81, the non-completion rate for men was consistently about five percentage points higher than that for women — broadly similar to the difference that was recorded by the Department of Education and Science (1992) for polytechnic and college students who had entered higher education in 1987 and strikingly similar to the difference in graduation rate found more recently by Astin et al. (1996) in the United States.

Intra-personal factors

Under this heading are grouped factors that relate to study styles, motivation, personality and the like. However, there are relatively few data which relate these specifically to completion or non-completion. Richardson (1995) used multiple regression, using completion of degree study of mature students as the dependent variable. He found that, for this group of students, successful completion was associated with greater age and with higher scores on the use of evidence and logic (from the Approaches to Study Inventory (ASI: Entwistle and Ramsden, 1983)), but with lower scores on the interrelationship of ideas. However, as Richardson notes, the findings may reflect the particular circumstances of his study since Kember and Harper (1987) had earlier found that subscales of the ASI *other than* the use of evidence and logic and the interrelationship of ideas were significant predictors of successful completion.

Motivation with respect to continuation or withdrawal is a variable that has been relatively little studied. Johnes (1990) did find, however, as an outcome of her survey of undergraduates from the 1979 cohort at Lancaster University who had not completed their degrees by 1985, that 6.1 per cent had lost interest and that a further 1.8 per cent had been unhappy with academic life. In a study of students seeking to enter higher education via routes which did not involve A-level examinations, Smith et al. (1996) show, through qualitative studies, the importance of motivation and self-confidence to success — a finding that accords with what many academics would say and which would seem to have considerable transfer value.

Preparedness for higher education was identified by Ozga and Sukhnandan (1997), in their study of non-completers from 'Campus University', as being of importance for (non-)completion. A relatively unprepared student may, as a result, lack the knowledge to make an appropriate choice of study programme; however, and as noted earlier, Ozga and Sukhnandan's results show that there was a high incidence of incompatibility between student and institution and/or programme even when the student appeared to have been well prepared for higher education. If choice of programme is poor, then there is likely to follow a negative impact on motivation.

Stress may be a contributory factor in non-completion. Humphrey and McCarthy et al. (1998) obtained 956 responses[14] of students at the University of Newcastle to a survey exploring the correlates of stress and showed that levels of stress amongst the respondents was higher than the average from the Household Panel Survey of 1992. Amongst their other findings were that the students' financial situations were unrelated to stress,[15] that students who felt less secure in their environment were more likely to be stressed and that perceptions of physical fitness and good personal health were associated with lower levels of stress. However, the most prominent correlate, as revealed by stepwise multiple regression, was that of good management of workload to a lower level of stress. Szulecka et al. (1987) had earlier suggested that psychiatric factors might account for at least one-third of student wastage from British universities — a rather startling finding which would seem to stand in need of corroboration.

Some studies from other countries

Comparisons within the United Kingdom national system are precarious because of differences in the way that studies have been conceived, in the operational measures that have been used, the variation in institutional type, and the extent to which the findings have become dated (given the rapid rate of change in higher education in recent years). When one seeks to cross national boundaries, comparisons become still more precarious because of the variation between national systems: contrast, for example, the differences in approach to participation and non-completion in the United Kingdom and — say — Italy.

Despite these difficulties, Moortgat (1996) made a brave but flawed attempt at a comparative study of five higher education systems in Europe — those of England, France, The Federal Republic of Germany, Italy, and the French community of Belgium (the case study of England is problematic in a number of methodological respects and is not considered further here). His difficulties were compounded by the necessity of drawing on data which had been produced in and about these systems for a variety of purposes, and hence were not commensurable. Moortgat showed that there was a high variation between these five countries in their non-completion rates, and his findings were augmented (with similar caveats regarding measurement) in an OECD study which also included Denmark and the Flemish community of Belgium (CERI, 1997, pp. 93–5, 118).

In France, where numbers expanded by half between 1982 and 1993, the graduation rate from higher education is reported as having risen from 35 per cent in 1984 to 44 per cent in 1993, although the proportion leaving higher education without any qualifications at all has remained virtually static at 30 per cent over the same period. Moortgat suggests that there are two main categories of student which are most at risk of withdrawing: holders of technical baccalaureates who opt for an inappropriate course, and students from poorer backgrounds who suffer from financial problems. The suggestion is made that an influx of students entering on the basis of vocational baccalaureates is likely to raise the non-completion rate in university education.

According to Moortgat, the non-completion rate[16] in the Federal Republic of Germany roughly doubled between 1974 and 1975 (when it was 12–16 per cent) and 1991–92 (29–31 per cent). Adding to the concern was the increase in the time taken before withdrawing: in Germany most universities adopted an assessment system in which a single examination was taken at the end of the programme, so there were no academic imperatives regarding failure at intermediate stages. Nor were there any pressures for students to complete within a given time. However, the Federal Government is reported as having recently recognized the need for radical reform in both the way that universities operate and also the permissible duration of study. Withdrawal is more likely for women than for men, for students from working class backgrounds than for students whose parents are university-educated, for students with vocational backgrounds, for students who seek to combine employment with study and for those whose grades on leaving school are low.

Moortgat quotes data from a study by Lewin (1995) which show the reasons given for withdrawal in samples of students in 1974–75 and 1993–94 (Table 2.3).

Table 2.3   Percentages of respondents citing the above reasons for withdrawal, ordered according to the 1993–94 findings

Reason	1974–75	1993–94
Demotivation regarding studies	36	73
Unsuitability of the course (content, teaching)	16	63
Attactive job offer (not requiring a degree)	12	53
Length of course and poor job prospects	14	49
Financial	15	38
Overwork	36	34
Family	14	18

Source: Lewin (1995), quoted by Moortgat (1996, p. 28).

Italy had, by the late 1980s, a non-completion rate approaching 64 per cent, which was attributed to open access to higher education. Moortgat claims that restrictions on entry in the 1990s are beginning to reduce this figure. Around half of the students fail their courses, whereas some 30 per cent seem to be 'phantom students' who appear to be engaged on the later stages of their courses for a number of years without actually completing them. Those who withdraw early, it is suggested, are weakly motivated (male students can postpone military service by entering higher education, and unemployment and peer pressure are also mentioned as stimuli to entry). On the other hand, those who withdraw later on may have personal or academic problems, or simply decide to make different life-choices. Non-completion is differentiated by gender: men are more likely than women to fail or withdraw for work-related reasons, whereas women are more than twice as likely as men not to complete because of reasons related to marriage or family. Moortgat quotes a study which points to a number of institutional influences on non-completion — lack of information, lack of advice and counselling, inadequate infrastructure for teaching and learning and a poor teacher/student ratio.

Moortgat reports that the number of students in the French community of Belgium had, by 1992, risen to nearly three times that of 1961. Against that background, the estimated withdrawal rate for non-university higher education was 38 per cent whereas for university education it had remained fairly stable between 23 and 27 per cent. The most successful group, as far as completion was concerned, was Belgian home-educated males — but 45 per cent of these students left without graduating. A study is reported which suggests that withdrawers tend to cite as criticisms (and not necessarily as actual influences on withdrawal) the lack of contact with teaching staff, unsuitable teaching methods, assessment procedures and programme content.

In Canada Johnson (1996) investigated, using a telephone questionnaire, the determinants of voluntary and involuntary withdrawal in a single-institution sample of 185 Arts, Education and Science students. Those required to withdraw tended to be younger and (not surprisingly, therefore) to have had less work experience. Voluntarily withdrawn Arts and Science students tended to have a greater proportion of graduate parents than did their involuntarily withdrawn peers. Those who had been required to withdraw had been less assiduous in fulfilling various academic expectations, the Arts students perhaps acting to stereotype by spending a considerably larger amount of their time in social activities. There was a greater tendency for the involuntarily withdrawn Arts and Science students, but not the Education students, to be dissatisfied with the quality of instruction. Johnson comments that a greater focus on pre-admission counselling might help to alleviate attrition.

In a previous study (which was mentioned earlier), Johnson and Buck investigated the reasons why students had withdrawn from a Canadian university. Of those required to withdraw, the vast majority of first responses stated the obvious — that their academic performance had been inadequate. The second responses were more illuminating and were grouped into four categories: academic behaviour/performance, personal/financial, attitude/personality and programme/administration. Of the responses, the most frequently mentioned were poor study habits and lack of commitment. Voluntary withdrawers provided lists of reasons from which no clear pattern emerged: the most frequently mentioned reason was the wrong choice of programme, but this was the case for only 9.2 per cent of the group.

The Australian work of McInnis et al. (1995), though on the first-year experience in higher education, is of some relevance since it deals with the period when students are at greatest risk of withdrawal. Commenting that the nature of the student body has changed in recent years (having expanded in a manner similar to that in the United Kingdom), they noted that only about half the students found their studies interesting, that a similar proportion felt that staff were enthusiastic about their subjects, that less than half felt that the staff were good at explaining, that over a quarter of the students worked in isolation (suggesting weaknesses in respect of Tinto's academic *and* social integration) and that nearly one-third of the students felt sufficiently disenchanted with their experience of higher education to consider seriously whether to defer their studies. School leavers were found to be the most problematic group of students, being less sure of their role than their older peers, less diligent in study (here there is a parallel with Johnson's (1996) involuntary withdrawers) and less oriented towards academic activity. One-third of these students admitted to being unready to choose a university course.

Postle et al. (n.d.), writing of Australian higher education in 1995, suggested that the job of the university had changed from half a century ago: now the aim was to ensure adequate standards for all rather than high standards for a few. In this context the process of teaching became important, since the imperative was to aim for student gain. In contributing to the same study Skuja (n.d.) showed that retention rates were influenced by demographic variables such as whether the student was indigenous to the country and the student's geographical remoteness (which are likely to co-vary), and the student's mode of study. As one might expect, full-time students' retention rates were higher than those for part-time or external students, and non-indigenous students' retention rates were from 10 to 24 per cent higher than those of indigenous students. Geographical remoteness was more likely to have an adverse effect on retention for indigenous than for non-indigenous students.

Earlier, Long et al. (1995, p. 13), reviewing the Australian literature on non-completion, reported that the reasons given by students for voluntary withdrawal appeared to fall within the following bands:

- problems with employment, 15–50 per cent;
- nature of the course, 20–35 per cent;
- health and chance events, 10–20 per cent;
- institutional factors, 5–20 per cent;
- financial difficulty, around 15 per cent; and
- family or other commitments, 5–15 per cent.

Students tended to give multiple reasons for withdrawal, the primary reason often being difficult to determine.

In the same academic (and general geographical) territory, Boddy (1996) has reported early outcomes from a longitudinal study of the student experience at the Victoria University of Wellington. She notes the impact of the greater competitive ethos in New Zealand higher education and records that less than 10 per cent of school career advisers were rated by the students as 'very helpful'. She speculates that perhaps up to 40 per cent of respondents had not chosen their major field of study positively (a student is obliged to make a choice in order to have an academic 'home') and that this indicates the lack of a clear commitment to a particular course of study. There is a concern underlying Boddy's work that there is a discrepancy between expectation and reality which is often exacerbated by — as she puts it — the 'selling of the sizzle not the sausage' (p. 7).

Some themes from the literature

What can usefully be extracted from this very disparate literature? With caution appropriate to its very varied nature and quality, it is probably not unreasonable to suggest that it allows the following inferences to be drawn. Withdrawal or failure tends to be more probable when:

- students' expectations are not met;
- students find that they have chosen 'the wrong programme'; and
- the student lacks commitment to, or interest in, the subject.

These three influences appear to be more potent for younger students, particularly school leavers, and raise the question of where the responsibility for the mismatch might lie.

Other circumstances which tend to lead to withdrawal or failure are those in which:

- the quality of teaching is poor;
- the academic culture is perceived by students as unsupportive (or even hostile);
- students find themselves in financial difficulty;
- the demands of other commitments — particularly the need to undertake employment — detract from studies (though note must be taken of the finding from the United States that students undertaking part-time employment *on campus* appear to have a lower incidence of withdrawal);
- the student is male (though this does not hold in all cultures);
- the student comes from a working class background; and
- the student enters with low academic (in the United Kingdom, A-level) grades.

It was noted by Pascarella and Terenzini (1991) in their review of studies from the United States that the more the student invested personally in his or her education, the more likely he or she was to complete the programme. Given changes that have taken place in the funding of students in the United Kingdom, this finding may have some transfer-value.

On a completely separate tack, Johnes and Taylor (1990a) demonstrated how problematic it is to use non-completion rates as a performance indicator.

One superordinate theme seems to come through the literature: the sheer difficulty of pinning down where the responsibility for non-completion might actually lie. Schools careers services, the students themselves, the institutions and their academic organizational units, and the national system of funding are amongst the possible loci. The lack of a reliable understanding should engender caution in any who might wish to use non-completion data for the purposes of sanction or reward.

Notes

1. As Pascarella and Terenzini (1991, p. 51) remark, it is doubtful whether such a statement actually constitutes a theory, as the term 'theory' is widely understood.
2. However, given that the focus of his theory is departure, the emphasis should perhaps be on the failure to integrate.
3. The authors acknowledge the need to test their approach in different institutional settings but seem rather sanguine about their response rate of 19 per cent.
4. Psychological state is also influenced by societal variables.
5. Some of this material can be found on the ERIC database.
6. Probably an overstatement when the effect appears likely to account for no more than 1 or 2 per cent of the variance in a number of outcome measures.
7. The corresponding percentage for students taking Humanities and Social Science majors was just under 30.
8. This has its origin in the Federal Right to Know Act which requires two-year institutions to report a three-year graduation rate, and four-year institutions to report a six-year graduation rate.
9. A study by Blumberg et al. (1997) of the 1988 cohort at the City University of New York produced findings that were in line with those of Astin et al. (1996).
10. Although Mexican American/Chicano men and Puerto Rican-American men marginally outperformed women.
11. High school grade proved to be the strongest predictor in regressions in which degree completion was the dependent variable.
12. Johnes (1990, p. 91) remarked that financial considerations were 'unlikely to be a prime cause of wastage in United Kingdom universities owing to the payment to most United Kingdom students of a maintenance grant . . .', but noted, presciently, that this might change with the introduction of student loans (at the time imminent).
13. The growth in the use of student loans during this period could also be a factor here.
14. The response rate was 49 per cent, a level which was probably achieved by delivering and collecting the survey forms by hand.
15. They suggest that debt is now a fact of life for students — but one whose implications for stress may reveal themselves later on in life as repayment becomes necessary.
16. This does not take into account students who re-enrol or transfer between institutions.

Chapter 3

Surveying the Domain

Orientation

Researchers are often constrained in their choice of method and this chapter opens by indicating the limits within which the research had to be undertaken. A general indication is then given of the scope of the research, and this is followed by a description of the actual survey methods (mail and telephone) that were used. A number of differences between the findings from the two different types of survey are noted, and a rationale is advanced for the approach that underpins the analyses in the succeeding chapters.

Choice of research method

The method chosen for a piece of research is strongly influenced by a number of considerations such as the resources and time available and the needs of a sponsor. Policy-related research generally requires some weight in statistics, lest policy development be open to the charge that it is being based on an inadequate foundation. Crudely, one might say that policy should not be based on a couple of anecdotes — though there are suspicions that at times reality approaches this, such as the investigations into academic standards in the United Kingdom that stemmed from a visit by the then Minister for Education, John Patten, to eastern Asia.

In this case, the main issues were the time available (just over one year) and the need of HEFCE to have data sufficiently robust for the underpinning of possible developments in policy. A longitudinal, and perhaps qualitative, approach, which would have allowed the way in which events combined to influence whether a student completed a programme of study, was therefore out of the question. The methodological decision was therefore more or less forced: a substantial sample of students who had left their studies would be surveyed by questionnaire in order to find out what the causes of their departure were. The pressure of time meant that no attempt would be made to interview students face to face: the work being conducted in parallel by Ozga and Sukhnandan (1997) would have the potential to allow some cross-referencing (albeit on different groups of students) to take place.

Questionnaires are not unproblematic. They tend to focus on what the researchers identify as the problem, decisions have to be made on a number of technical issues[1] and, in the case of students who had already left their programmes of study, responses might be affected by the passage of time, the need to present the reasons for departure in the best light, and so on. The interpretation of data would need to acknowledge that bias would probably be inherent and to some extent unquantifiable.

The students involved in the survey

The students involved in the research were from six institutions in the north-west of England, and who were recorded as having left their programmes prematurely during, or at the end of, the academic year 1994–95. The research was limited to those who were funded through HEFCE. The choice of the academic year 1994–95 allowed an estimate to be made of the proportion which had returned to study by the autumn of 1996 — a matter of consider-able importance in estimating the cost of non-completion. The institutions involved were two pre-1992 universities, two post-1992 universities and two institutions from the colleges sector, which together accounted for about 7.5 per cent of student enrolments in England, in full-time, sandwich and part-time modes. The total number of 'non-completers' (according to institutional records) was 5512, of whom 4627 were recorded as having been full-time or sandwich students and 766 as part-time students.

The opportunity arose to conduct, on a self-financed basis, a repeat survey in five[2] of the six original institutions with the students who were recorded as having left their programmes during, or at the end of, the academic year 1995–96. The total number of students to whom questionnaires were sent was 4461, of whom 2600 had studied in full-time or sandwich mode and 1387 had studied in part-time mode. It is unclear why part-time student withdrawals were more numerous than in the previous academic year.

The survey instruments

The main survey instrument was a six-page questionnaire whose responses could be processed on an optical mark reader. This was used, in almost exactly the same form, with the students who had left prematurely in each of the academic years 1994–95 and 1995–96. The response rate from the mail surveys was around 20 per cent, broadly consistent with the literature for similar studies, but low enough to cause concern that there might be significant bias in the responses. It was decided, in respect of those who had left full-time and sandwich programmes in 1994–95, to follow up the mail survey with a telephone survey of non-respondents in order to increase the response rate. For this purpose, a truncated version of the mail survey was used.

The mail questionnaires

The mail questionnaire was divided into five main sections. Section A solicited details of the institution that the student had attended, the qualifications which he or she had possessed at entry, the route by which he or she had enrolled and some outline details of the programme of study. The student was also asked what his or her mode of study had been (full-time, sandwich or part-time) and whether he or she had changed mode of study prior to withdrawal. An invitation was extended to indicate what the intended length of the study programme was and, depending on the answers to the questions relating to mode of study, to indicate how much of the programme had been completed prior to withdrawal.[3]

Section B asked the respondent to indicate, on a four-point scale, the extent to which each of 36 supplied possible influences had impacted on his or her withdrawal: the scale points were labelled 'no influence', 'a little influence', 'a moderate influence' and 'a considerable influence'. This section of the questionnaire was itself divided into three subsections which dealt with matters relating to the programme of study, the institution and its provision of facilities, and personal considerations. Some possible influences that, a priori, seemed likely to apply to only a minority of respondents, such as pregnancy or bereavement, were not included in the list of provided possible influences. However, provision was made for the respondent to write down any influences that had not been covered in the questionnaire and/or to expand on those that had already been noted. (The second version of this questionnaire, on the students who left in 1995–96, used 39, rather than 36, supplied possible influences.)

Section C asked for some personal information: gender, age at the commencement of the programme, ethnic background (using the categories employed by UCAS in its admissions system) and the social class to which the student felt he or she belonged. The respondent was also asked to indicate whether he or she had a disability and, if so, what the disability was and the extent to which he or she was satisfied with the institution's provision for it.

Section D asked whether the student had already returned to study and, if he or she had not returned, whether the intention was to do so in the near future. If either of these produced an affirmative response, the student was asked whether the study programme was (or would be) similar or different, whether a year's-worth of study would be being repeated, and whether he or she had returned or intended to return to the same or a different institution.

Section E requested information about whether the student had sought advice before withdrawing and, if so, from whom that advice had been sought. A concluding open-response question asked the student to indicate what more might have been done by the institution to support the completion of the study programme. Full details of the first questionnaire can be found in Yorke et al. (1997b).

The questionnaires were mailed from the students' home institutions, together with a covering letter describing the nature of the project and explaining why the responses would be important to the sector and to future students.[4] A 'Freepost' envelope was also included for the questionnaire's return. The vast majority of responses were received by the relevant deadline, but some responses trickled in afterwards in sufficient time to be entered into the analysis.

The response rates for the three types of institution were 24.5 per cent (pre-1992 universities), 20.0 per cent (post-1992 universities) and 17.4 per cent (colleges): overall the response rate was 20.4 per cent. For full-time and sandwich students overall, the response rate was 22.5 per cent, and for part-time students 15.2 per cent.[5]

The overall response rate for full-time and sandwich students is probably consistent with response rates of 25–30 per cent noted in the literature for surveys undertaken rather closer to the time of the students' withdrawal.[6] That for part-time students may be being deflated because of the greater difficulty in identifying unambiguously whether a student has actually withdrawn: questionnaires may have been sent to students who considered themselves to be continuing with their studies (and hence did not respond) even though the institutional records may have indicated to the contrary.

The telephone survey

Given the much greater numbers of full-time and sandwich students compared with part-time students, the extent to which the first two groups were supported through national funding mechanisms and the flexibility with which the latter could conduct their studies, the telephone survey of non-respondent leavers from 1994–95 was limited to full-time and sandwich students.

The full mail questionnaire would have been too long for a telephone survey and so decisions had to be made regarding the questions which could be omitted without damaging the general intentions of the survey or the need to test whether the non-respondents to the mail survey were in some ways different from the respondents. Accordingly, a number of points of detail were eliminated: those relating to the nature of the student's entry qualification, change of mode of study (very few of the mail survey respondents had changed mode), ethnicity, social class, disability and the soliciting of advice prior to withdrawal. The question regarding the nature of the degree programme was simplified to a dichotomy — single-subject programme or a programme containing more than one subject of study. Trials with the shortened questionnaire indicated that it could be completed in around ten minutes provided that the respondent was not unduly talkative.

The telephone survey was run over eight evenings from Liverpool John Moores University. Nineteen students from the Job Shop run by the Students' Union at the university were recruited to undertake the survey. The interviewers had all had experience of some sort in dealing with the general public; for example, some had undertaken telephone interviewing previously and others had had employment in the field of consumer services.

The mail survey responses had provided an under-representation of certain categories of students (for example, men aged under 21 at one of the post-1992 universities and women aged 21 and above in one of the colleges) and hence the telephone survey offered an opportunity to correct this. The telephone survey was therefore stratified with reference to the level of response to the mail survey. The interviewers were provided with a protocol for their work. This was used to steer the interviews but not to straitjacket their questioning, as it was felt that respondents would be more forthcoming if a more conversational approach was adapted for the interview.[7] The responses to the telephone survey did achieve a distribution roughly as required but were limited in attaining the precise balance desired because of the unavailability of information from one institutional database,[8] an inability to contact former students (because many telephone numbers were no longer current[9] or the students had moved away) and an unwillingness on the part of a small number of students to respond.

Some students made a point of welcoming the telephone survey since they found it an opportunity to say things about their experience of higher education that they had hitherto felt unable to mention. Some of the interviews, as a result, took considerably longer than the ten minutes anticipated. In a couple of instances it was possible to assist the respondent to deal with ongoing difficulties associated with the withdrawal — for example, by suggesting ways in which a former student might obtain the financial support needed and by helping a parent and an institution to resolve a grievance that had got stuck in the latter's system. On the other hand, the telephone survey was not welcomed by a handful of respondents.

The telephone survey raised the overall response rate for full-time and sandwich students who withdrew in 1994–95 from 20.7 per cent to 31.9 per cent, and rectified to a fair extent the unevenness that was apparent in the responses from the mail survey. The true response rates are likely to have been higher than those reported here, because a number of respondents indicated that they had not left their institutions and that the institutional record system was in error as far as they were concerned.

Differences between the findings from the mail and
telephone surveys of those who left in 1994–95

The returns from the mail and telephone surveys for the 1994–95 'non-completers' showed a number of differences that were significant at at least the .01 level (see Appendix 2). There was a significantly greater proportion of students who had entered higher education via Clearing in the telephone survey (37.4 per cent compared with 25.7 per cent). There were no significant differences between the two groups of respondents as far as dichotomized programme type (single v. multiple subject), dichotomized entry qualifications

(A-level only v. not A-level only). About three-quarters of each group had returned, or intended to return, to higher education, though the proportion of actual 'returners' was higher in the mail survey group (just over 60 per cent against just under 50 per cent for the telephone survey group). It might have been thought that those who responded to the mailed survey could have done so because they 'felt relatively good' about their decisions to withdraw and re-engage: however, if intentionality about returning is taken into account, there seems to be little ground for making a distinction between the two groups.

As regards influences on withdrawal, significant differences between the two groups related to two main sets of variables — the student's satisfaction with his or her experience of the programme entered and followed, and matters related to finance. Non-significant differences were found in respect of variables that could be construed more as 'background to engagement in higher education', such as personal health, matters relating to family and friends and comfortableness with the local environment. In the non-significant group of variables, there appeared only two relating to the student experience of the institution and over which the institution could exercise control — support of staff outside timetabled hours and the institution not being as expected.

Taken in the round, these findings suggest that the differences are connected with the relationship between the student and the programme and that there is no identifiable difference between the two groups on criteria that can be construed as 'extra-institutional' save for finance and related matters. Where significant differences do exist (other than those that were finance-related), they generally suggest that institutional factors had a stronger influence on withdrawal for the telephone survey respondents than for the mail survey respondents. The differences are, for some variables, quite marked — the frequency of citing by the telephone respondents often being of the order of 50 per cent higher than that of the mail survey respondents. The largest of the proportionate differences was where the programme was adjudged not to be relevant to the student's career.

There are at least two potential reasons for the differences between the two survey approaches. The differences could reflect true differences between the respondents and non-respondents to the mail survey. It could be that those who responded to the mail questionnaire tended to 'feel better' about their experience of higher education than those who only responded when subsequently contacted by telephone. Alternatively, some form of social desirability bias could have resulted from the way in which the telephonist/respondent interactions took place.

The higher proportion of telephone respondents who entered via Clearing may have accounted for the differences observed in variables such as 'chose the wrong field of study' and 'lack of commitment to the programme'. This is, however, inconsistent with the fact that, for the body of respondents as a whole, whether or not they entered higher education through the Clearing procedure seemed to make little difference to the general run of responses.

The finding may be confounded by some confusion on the part of respondents as to whether they had actually entered via Clearing.

Analysis

A compromise

The first mail survey and the follow-up telephone survey produced very similar *patterns* when the data for the full-time and sandwich (FT/SW) students were factor analysed, even though the intensities of response from the telephone respondents were markedly higher for some of the variables in Section B. The second mail survey showed a very similar response pattern to the first.

The decision was made to combine the results from the three surveys of FT/SW students (despite their different bases) in order to allow various sub-group analyses to have reasonable numbers in the analytical cells. Considerable interest resides in the sub-group analyses, and particularly in that relating to academic subject category. In combining the data, it is acknowledged that methodological purity is being traded off against practical utility.

The combined set of three data files was used in most of the analyses relating to full-time and sandwich students; where questions were not asked of the telephone respondents, the analyses refer to the mail survey respondents only. The outcomes of the analyses are given in Chapter 4.

For the part-time students, only mail questionnaire data were available, and the analyses in Chapter 5 refer to the combined data for 1994–95 and 1995–96.

Methods

Data were analysed via SPSS, the simpler analyses using descriptive statistics and cross-tabulations. Responses to the four-point scales relating to the influences on withdrawal were recoded such that 'no influence' or 'little influence' were coded 0 and 'moderate influence' and 'considerable influence' were coded 1. This transformation produced an index of influence for each of the provided variables which ranged from 0 to 1 and gives values whose weight is easy to grasp and which, when placed in a table, enable relativities to be appreciated easily. The dichotomized data were used in a number of exploratory analyses of the differences between sub-groups of respondents (e.g. with respect to gender, age, institutional type). Given that the data were 'cut' in a number of directions, there is a risk of over-interpreting the significance of differences, hence the significances quoted are taken as suggestive rather than definitive.

The data matrix of provided possible influences (scored from 1 to 4) by number of cases was subjected to principal components analysis with varimax rotation in order to produce a manageable number of meaningful factors. This method permitted Anderson-Rubin factor scores to be computed, enabling 'broad-brush' summaries of the main features of the data to be produced.[10]

Notes

1. For an example of decision making related to questionnaires, see Yorke (1996b, pp. 109–12).
2. On this occasion a 50 per cent sample was drawn from the largest of the institutions involved because of limitations on the resources available.
3. In the case of a full-time or sandwich programme, the number of years completed prior to withdrawal was asked. Where the student had been undertaking part-time study or had switched mode, he or she was asked to give an estimate of the proportion of the programme that had been completed prior to withdrawal.
4. The project's Liverpool address was stamped on the back of the envelopes in order to enable undeliverable envelopes to be returned.
5. These figures make allowance for questionnaires returned undelivered and for responses indicating that institutional records had wrongly recorded students as having withdrawn.
6. Thomas et al. (1996) report a response rate of just under 20 per cent from a mail survey conducted a similar time after the students had withdrawn. A similar response rate was obtained by Fennell (1997).
7. There is a trade-off here between replicability of the interview and the potential maximization of the response. In this project, the decision was to tend towards the latter. Dillman (1978) takes a different view on this issue. The literature offers surprisingly little guidance on the relative effects of different methodological procedures, since the circumstances of studies have varied widely. Sudman and Bradburn (1974) suggest that the nature of the task and the conditions under which it is performed are likely to have a greater effect on the outcomes than interviewer characteristics, and that social desirability is more likely to intrude when the topic of the interview is of some sensitivity.
8. This was due to a transition from an earlier database to a new one.
9. Recent developments in the provision of telephone services seem to have resulted in many subscribers switching from BT to an alternative provider, with the effect that many telephone numbers on the institutional database were no longer available. In addition, a number of calls were answered by an answering machine. In these circumstances the interviewers were instructed not to spend time leaving messages but to note the possibility that at a later date a further call might elicit a live response. Some students indicated that they would be available at a later date to be interviewed but for various reasons contact was not made with them.
10. Some might wish to argue that the non-parametric Spearman rho correlation coefficient should have been computed and the Spearman correlation matrix input into the principal components analysis: details of this procedure can be found in SPSS (1993, p. 508ff (and particularly pp. 512–13)) and Norusis (1994, pp. 311–14). In fact, the Pearson product-moment coefficient r is little affected by non-normality of distribution provided — as is the case here — that the *shapes* of the distributions are homogeneous (DuBois, 1963; Youngman, 1976). In practice, the numerical differences between r and *rho* for these data were very small, and principal components analyses using the Pearson and Spearman methods gave remarkably similar results. The Pearson method was chosen because it produced an output almost identical to that produced using the Spearman method and because it had the distinct advantage of allowing factor scores to be computed — an option that was not available via the Spearman route.

Chapter 4

Money, Choice and Quality: Why Full-time and Sandwich Students Leave Early

Orientation

This chapter gives the outcomes of the analyses of the data from the full-time and sandwich students. The first section describes the students' background characteristics, and this is followed by an analysis of the influences on their withdrawals. Further analysis revealed six factors that subsume the much longer list of possible influences on withdrawal, and these are elaborated with comments from the students, some of which are quite colourful. The data set is 'cut' in a number of ways in exploratory analyses which suggest where differences between sub-groups (based on characteristics such as age and gender) might lie. A short section then indicates the extent to which the students sought advice from within the institution before leaving. The chapter ends with an analysis of the (surprising) extent to which the withdrawn students had returned to study.

What were the backgrounds of the respondents?

The 2151 full-time and sandwich students who responded to the surveys contained roughly equal numbers of men and women, both groups being dominated by those who had entered higher education more or less straight from school.[1] As far as their self-reporting of social class was concerned, the respondents were evenly divided between working class, 'no particular class' and middle/upper class. Over 90 per cent of the respondents described themselves as white. Seven per cent described themselves as having a disability, the disabilities covering a range of more than a dozen forms.

There were more respondents from the post-1992 universities (1291) than pre-1992 universities (528) and colleges (325), reflecting various factors such as institutional size, institutional policy regarding admission and student background characteristics. In each type of institution, a majority of respondents had entered on the basis of A-level examination results, the highest proportion of such students (72 per cent) being found in the pre-1992 universities. As would be expected, the pre-1992 universities tended to have enrolled students with higher A-level points scores. There were, from the post-1992 universities and colleges, higher proportions of respondents aged 21 and above than from the pre-1992 universities; this is consistent with sectoral demographics.

About half of the respondents said that they had been pursuing a single-subject programme, and about 40 per cent had been following a programme involving two or more subjects. The vast majority of respondents were following a degree-level programme.

The distribution of responses by HEFCE Academic Subject Category and three unofficial hybrid categories (50, 51, 52) constructed for the purposes of analysis was as in Table 4.1.

Table 4.1   Distribution of responses by ASC and unofficial 'hybrid' ASC

ASC	Subjects subsumed	Number of respondents	Percentage
1	Clinical and Pre-Clinical	15	0.7
2	Subjects and Professions Allied to Medicine	103	5.2
3	Science	264	13.4
4	Engineering and Technology	195	9.9
5	Built Environment	68	3.5
6	Mathematics, Information Technology and Computing	126	6.4
7	Business and Management	233	11.9
8	Social Science	219	11.2
9	Humanities	286	14.6
10	Art, Design and Performing Arts	104	5.3
11	Education	121	6.2
50	Mixed Arts-based	92	4.7
51	Mixed Science-based	56	2.9
52	Mixed Arts-based and Science-based	82	4.2

For the mail surveys only, students were asked to provide details of their entry qualifications in order that an assessment could be made of the extent to which these matched the programme of study for which they had enrolled. This entailed subjective judgement in a number of cases, particularly where a student had A-level passes in both science and humanities/arts subjects and where the subject being studied had no analogous subject at A-level. Matches were classified as 'good', 'partial' and 'weak'. A 'good' match between entry qualifications and programme was identified in 1108 cases, a 'partial' match in 265 and a 'weak' match in 76.

The withdrawers were asked to indicate the point at which they had left the programme on which they had embarked. Nearly half (47 per cent) had left *during* the first year of study, and a further 38 per cent left at the end of the first year or during the second year.[2]

Influences on withdrawal

The influences on withdrawal that were acknowledged by the respondents as 'moderate' or 'considerable' are shown in Table 4.2.

Table 4.2 Influences on the decision to withdraw, as cited by 2151 full-time and sandwich students

Variable	Percentage indicating moderate or considerable influence
Chose wrong field of study	39
Lack of commitment to the programme	38
Financial problems	37
Programme not what I expected	37
Teaching did not suit me	31
Insufficient academic progress	30
Needed a break from education	28
Programme organization	27
Inadequate staff support outside timetable	24
Lack of personal support from staff	24
Quality of teaching	23
Programme not relevant to my career	23
Emotional difficulties with others	23
Personal health problems	23
Stress related to the programme	22
Difficulty of the programme	21
Institution not what I expected	19
Accommodation problems	18
Workload too heavy	17
Lack of study skills	17
Class sizes too large	16
Demands of employment whilst studying	15
Dislike of city/town	15
Needs of dependants	15
Lack of personal support from students	15
Travel difficulties	15
Lack of personal support from family	12
Timetabling did not suit	11
Homesickness	11
Taking up employment*	10
Fear of crime	10
Difficulty in making friends	9
Institutional computing facilities	9
Institutional provision of social facilities	9
Institutional library provision	8
Institutional provision of specialist equipment	7
Problems with drugs/alcohol	7
Bereavement of someone close*	6
Pregnancy (self or partner's)*	6

Note: Valid numbers per item range from 2085 to 2147, with the exception of the three asterisked items which were only included in the 1995–96 mail survey and attracted between 612 and 673 responses.

Table 4.2 shows that, for full-time and sandwich student 'withdrawers', the dominant influences cited in respect of premature departure relate to the wrong choice of field of study and financial difficulty, with aspects of teaching and learning slightly less to the fore. Aspects of institutional provision were infrequently cited as influences on withdrawal.

Factor analysis

A long list of influences is not particularly helpful to those who have to deter-mine policy and instigate action, and in any case there is overlap between the influences. In order to reduce the complexity of Table 4.2, the matrix of responses to the 36 supplied possible influences was subjected to principal components analysis with varimax rotation.[3] This produced a six-factor solu-tion which accounted for 48.5 per cent of the variance (Appendix 3(a)). Anderson-Rubin scores were produced by the analysis for each of the identi-fied factors in order to facilitate 'broad-brush' comparisons in sub-analyses.

Table 4.3   Labels for the six factors

Factor no.	Per cent variance	Label
1	19.6	Poor quality of the student experience
2	8.0	Inability to cope with the demands of the programme
3	6.6	Unhappiness with the social environment
4	5.9	Wrong choice of programme
5	4.6	Matters related to financial need
6	3.8	Dissatisfaction with aspects of institutional provision

The six factors are as shown in Table 4.3. Care should be taken when reading Table 4.3 not to confuse the percentage of the variance explained by a factor and the salience of the items that load heavily on it. That this caution is necessary is illustrated by Factors 4 and 5: reference back to Table 4.2 shows that choice of the wrong field of study and financial problems were respec-tively the first and third most frequently cited influences on withdrawal.

The six factors: an elaboration

A qualitative elaboration of the six factors is given below in which additional comments offered by respondents have been included by way of illustration (though they cannot be taken as representative of the body of respondents as a whole).

Factor 1: Poor quality of the student experience

The main components of this factor relate to the quality of the teaching, the level of support given by staff and the organization of the programme.

Few additional comments were made by respondents regarding the detail of their dissatisfaction with the teaching that they had received.[4] Some reported disliking lectures (for various reasons), and one respondent was unhappy about the lack of small discussion groups:

> The lack of small discussion groups was the worst part, it was all so anonymous.
>
> > (Humanities)

It is not clear whether, for this student, the problem was the lack of discussion groups or that the discussion groups were large. Another student picked out the latter issue:

> Tutorials had 25+ students only enabling the very self-confident to dominate the proceedings.
>
> > (Social Sciences)

A further student drew attention to the forbidding character of seminar groups as experienced:

> Did not like the structure of the seminar groups as I found them extremely intimidating and cold.
>
> > (Social Sciences)

Lack of staff support within and outwith the timetable was a major concern for some respondents.

> BTEC [entry] students such as myself were expected to be at the same standard as A level students mathematically — this is seldom the case. Support from staff was minimal. This led to lack of commitment which led to lack of interest.
>
> > (Engineering)

> During my 2 yrs at [university] found many of the lecturers unsupportive and extremely unhelpful (some completely opposite). I was the only female on course and felt unwelcomed from the lecturers — chauvinistic attitude.
>
> > (Science)

> I completed an access course prior to attending [university] where the staff were really helpful and knew you on a 1 to 1 basis. At university this wasn't the case and [. . .] I couldn't cope with the workload with no tutorial support.
>
> > (Diploma in Higher Education)

> Academic staff, on occasions, had a tendency to project themselves as being very pushed for time, stressed out and could not fit you into their timetable of work. No matter who you turned to, or when you sought [sic] someone's aid, they seemed to be busy.
>
> > (Science)

Programme organization was a significant weakness for some.

> Course I attended was the 1st yr they offered it and it was very disorganised.
>
> > (Technology)

> Staffing horrendous, no time management etc.
>
> > (Design)

Factor 2: Inability to cope with the demands of the programme

This factor is dominated by stress related to the programme, the difficulty of the programme and the weight of the workload. Loading a little less heavily on this factor are the lack of study skills (which could be causally related to both programme difficulty and stress) and the lack of personal support from students. Insufficient academic progress also loads on this factor, but — not surprisingly — loads almost equally on Factor 4 which reflects the choice of the wrong field of study.

Respondents provided few additional comments which bear on this factor. The matter most commented upon was that of difficulties with fellow students, where characteristics such as age, class and ethnicity appear to have left students feeling isolated and unsupported by their peers. More than one mature student commented on the difficulty of communicating with those who had come into higher education from school. Occasionally matters appear to have been worse: one student claimed to have been

> Basically bullied out of [institution] . . .
>
> (Humanities)

because her accent appeared to mark her as different from the rest of the group. Class tension pulled in the opposite direction for a working class student at a pre-1992 university:

> I think my background [. . .] had a considerable influence. I am from a work-ing class northern family and often felt alone and inferior because of this. Didn't have much in common with other students.
>
> (Languages)

Factor 3: Unhappiness with the social environment

Under this factor are found the dislike of the city or town in which the institu-tion was located, homesickness, problems with accommodation, fear of crime and difficulty in making friends. The last of these overlaps to some extent with the perceived lack of support from peers which appeared in Factor 2.

Respondents were prepared to elaborate much more for this factor than for others about relevant items, perhaps because some of the items loading on other factors were self-evident and needed no elaboration (for example, insufficient academic progress and weight of the workload). There seemed, on the part of some, a need to explain what had happened in the local environ-ment to precipitate their departure:

> I found [city] to be a depressing and violent place. While I was there 2 flatmates were hospitalised outside the flats and locals tried (unsuccessfully) to literally kick our front door down on 4 separate occasions.
>
> (Business)

> I was threatened by a knife at [. . .] station early in my course. [. . .] Also I missed my family, friends and home town enormously. I hated the place.
>
> > (Engineering)

> In Feb '95 I was robbed at gunpoint close to the house I was living in. I was also burgled twice. Crime was a part of my life during my 1st year at the institution. It caused me to dislike the city — not the institution — and [I] decided it better to move to another institution.
>
> > (Business)

> Disliked [city] due to crime. After six burglaries and ten vandalism attacks on my house I was attacked by 5–6 armed (gun) 14–16 year olds who stole all my stuff again!
>
> > (Medicine)

In contrast, some students who were based at outlying sites relatively inaccessible to the city were dissatisfied because they did not have access to the city's social life. Some pointed out that they had not realized that their programme would be run on an outlying site and implied that there had been, on the part of the relevant institution's promotional material, some economy with the truth.

Other respondents commented explicitly on difficulties that they had experienced with their accommodation.

> Living in hall of residence made learning and studying difficult.
>
> > (Nursing)

> Accommodation was very small and inadequate, like being in prison. You need privacy and it was impossible. Maybe if I found my own place it would have helped.
>
> > (Combined Studies)

> . . . I lived in halls which interfered with my private life. People who ran these halls went through our private belongings and restricted our spare time making it difficult for us to live there and we couldn't move out because of contract.
>
> > (Science)

> I was physically assaulted by my landlord.
>
> > (Engineering)

Factor 4: Wrong choice of programme

This factor subsumes the wrong choice of study programme, the discovery that the programme was not what had been expected, the lack of relevance to the student's intended career and the lack of commitment to the programme.

Comments indicated that a lack of clear sense of purpose and the expectations of others had played a significant part, for some respondents, in a poor initial decision regarding the programme of study.

> I was 18 years old, couldn't wait to leave home and had bad A-level grades. I got accepted on the first degree course I could. I didn't really have much direction.
>
> (Combined Science and Technology)

> I had no idea what I wanted to do after my A-levels & was advised to do Sociology as it was a general subject that could lead to many professions. Not only did I dislike the course, I was pushed into Uni by my parents . . .
>
> (Social Sciences)

> The degree I had chosen I knew was wrong before I went to the university. I was given very pressured advice from my former institution.
>
> (Humanities)

> Definitely went to University because I had always assumed the route school–uni–job and although I wasn't pressured, it was expected by school, friends, family, even myself. I re-applied this year (3 yrs after school) as I want to study for a degree and not just go to University.
>
> (Mathematics)

> Disinterest in the course, should have chosen a different one.
>
> (Science)

Others were taken by surprise regarding the nature of the programme on to which they had enrolled, some because of lack of information and some because of alleged misinformation.

> [My] Mathematics not up to the standard required. It was very difficult and the course content was not explained before I embarked on it.
>
> (Engineering)

> Unfortunately, I was led to believe by [institution] tutors on Open Day, that the course was perfectly suited to my needs and requirements. This wasn't the case despite my reiteration of what I wanted.
>
> (Technology)

> The course was totally different to the explanation in the prospectus [. . .] no open day or interviews were held.
>
> (Business)

A few respondents commented that the programme on which they had enrolled was simply insufficiently relevant to their intended career needs.

> There were too many subjects within the course that had no relevance to [industry], which when looking at these subjects in the actual industry they would not be undertaken by a [specialism] manager.
>
> (Production Management)

This student took up a position in the industry concerned, feeling that it would be preferable to be learning 'on the job', and claimed that this course of action had paid off. Another student who had enrolled on an overtly vocational course commented critically on the lack of 'hands-on' practicality in the curriculum.

Lack of commitment, not surprisingly, appears in this factor, and comments showed an overlap with other items, for example:

> I felt I had arrived at University because it was the easiest option and what had always been expected of me. I wasn't passionate about it.
>
> (Humanities)

Factor 5: Matters related to financial need

Financial problems have, as primary correlates, the demands of employment whilst studying and the needs of dependants. The lack of personal support from the family may in some cases be directly related to emotional difficulties with others. It is less clear why travel difficulties should load on to this factor, though a few students did comment on the expense of having to travel into the institution from a moderately distant location — for instance:

> In an attempt to cut costs and stay on course, I moved home and travelled daily to [city] which proved in the end too much.
>
> (Social Sciences)

For some students, fear of debt was a potent stimulus towards withdrawal.

> My main reason for leaving was finance. I soon realised that once I had paid for my rent for the year, I would have no money left. Didn't want to leave the university owing '000s of £. So got a job.
>
> (Humanities)

> One of my reasons for leaving was a financial one. I was terrified and completely panicked by the debt I would run up over the 3 years.
>
> (Combined Studies)

Some financial difficulties are self-induced and have inevitable knock-on effects, judging by the following comment:

I spent all my money too quickly and on the wrong things (going out and drink-
ing instead of paying my Hall fees). This contributed to my work slipping.
After missing so many lectures and seminars I was too scared to go any more.

(Humanities)

The cross-linking between financial difficulty and other influences on
withdrawal is exemplified in the following:

As a mature age student, I had a family to feed and a mortgage to pay. I had
found part-time work in the evenings but this was not enough and when the
chance to work full-time came along I took it.

(Computing)

. . . I was forced to work PT which ate into my studying time and my relaxa-
tion time. This generated a lot of stress for me [. . .]. My commitment to the
course was affected. I didn't feel that studying an Art degree subject with
little career/job assurance justified the severe three-year struggle required to
achieve it.

(Art and Design)

Young children made it difficult for one student:

As I have young children, who at the time were only aged 4 and 2, the net
result was I could not study sufficiently at home to complete or catch up on
my work.

(Engineering)

Factor 6: Dissatisfaction with aspects of institutional provision

This factor is fairly tightly defined and covers the provision of library, computing and specialist equipment resources and social facilities. For some students,
disproportionately those entering through the 'Clearing' process, the institution
itself turned out not to have been as the intending student had anticipated.

Few additional comments were provided to illuminate how the respondents had been influenced by their dissatisfaction to withdraw. Only where the
institution turned out not to have been what the student had expected were
comments made. In many cases the dissatisfaction related to the geographical
location of the programme (as noted in respect of Factor 3 above), but for a
small number the characteristics of the institution came as a shock:

I felt overwhelmed by the size of [university] — like a small fish in a big pond.
I felt isolated and scared . . .

(Humanities)

[Institution] had the 'feel' of a technical college dispensing degrees rather than a university.

(Engineering)

Exploratory analyses

The complexity of the collected data invited further exploratory analyses in order to try to identify the background variables most likely to be influencing withdrawal. Accordingly, a series of sub-group comparisons was undertaken.[5] These are reported below, using factor scores derived from the factor analyses. The factor scores provide a way of comparing groups in broad terms, inevitably losing some precision in the process. Fuller details of the statistically significant comparisons are given in the tables collated in Appendix 4.

Age

A dichotomous division of the responses according to age on entry to the programme (under 21, and 21 and over) gave rise to significant differences in respect of Factors 3, 4 and 5. In their withdrawal, the younger respondents were influenced more than their older peers by the wrong choice of programme and unhappiness with the social environment whereas they were less influenced by matters relating to financial need.

The finer-grained analyses presented in Appendix 4(c) show, *inter alia*, that younger students were roughly twice as likely as their older peers to have been influenced in their withdrawal by the wrong choice of the programme and the consequential loss of commitment. They were also more likely to have experienced difficulties with accommodation, to have feared crime, to have disliked the city or town in which they were studying and to have been homesick. There is perhaps implicit in these findings a hint of greater unpreparedness in the younger students for the vicissitudes of living away from home — a matter that the charity Shelter has sought to rectify through the provision of a pack of relevant educational materials to all secondary schools.

On the other hand, the older students, in addition to having a greater incidence of financial difficulty, suffered from the demands of employment whilst studying and from various difficulties with those who were close to them.

Some of the differences may in large part be attributable to the greater 'worldly-wiseness' of the older students who are likely to have come to terms with a number of the problems that appear to have precipitated the withdrawal of the younger students. Older students, who will in the main have spent some years out of full-time education, will have had more time to reflect on what they wanted to do and on the matters that needed to be arranged in order to bring their desires to fruition. Set against this, however, the older students are more likely to have family responsibilities of various kinds and, of all the possible influences on their withdrawal, financial problems are by far the most commonly cited.

Gender

There were a number of differences between male and female students as far as influences on withdrawal were concerned, which showed up at the gross levels of Factors 3, 4 and 5. Men were more likely than women to have been influenced by a combination of variables relating to having made the wrong choice of programme and to have found financial need an influence on their withdrawal. In contrast, women were more likely than men to have been unhappy with aspects of the social environment.

At the finer-grained level of analysis, men and women showed an equal incidence of having made the wrong choice of field of study, but differences seem to have shown themselves in the way that they accommodated to the wrongness of their choice — thus explaining the gender difference at the gross level of Factor 4. Men were half as likely again as women to cite their lack of commitment as an influence on withdrawal, and there were smaller differences in the same direction regarding the need for a break from education and the programme not being relevant to their career. Men reported more often than women that they had made insufficient academic progress, that they lacked study skills and that they found the programme difficult. There seems to have been a collection of influences at work here, to a greater extent on men than on women, that ties together wrongness of choice, lack of commitment, lack of ability to cope with academic demand and lack of academic progress.

Men were also half as likely again as women to cite the importance of financial problems, a difference that was reflected to a lesser extent in the demands of employment (presumably to rectify the problem) whilst studying.

Women cited more often than men personal health, pregnancy,[6] emotional difficulties with others and homesickness. They also cited more often than men the needs of dependants. Regarding this, sub-analysis threw up an interesting finding: when the dichotomized level of influence on the decision to withdraw (none/little v. moderate/considerable) was cross-tabulated with age and gender, it became apparent that the older the withdrawer, the greater appeared to be the likelihood that he or she would cite the needs of dependants as being influential.[7] Although the numbers of students who were aged over 24 were small, there is a clear indication that, beyond the age of 24, there is a disproportionate number of women who cite the needs of dependants as bearing on their decision to withdraw.

Social class

The question about social class was asked in the mail surveys but not the telephone survey; the findings are therefore based on 1584 definite responses. When these responses were divided according to self-reported social class,[8] there were marked differences on matters relating to finance-related items. Working class students reported more often than middle class students, and students of 'no particular class' more often than middle/upper class students, that financial problems had exerted a moderate or considerable influence on their withdrawal. A similar gradation was evident with respect to the demands of employment whilst studying. Travel difficulties also exhibited this gradation, but here it is unclear whether this relates to the costs associated with travel or to the freedom of movement allowed by the possession of a vehicle.

Middle/upper class students more than students of 'no particular class' and working class students reported more frequently as influences on their departure the choice of the wrong field of study and the dislike of the city or town in which the higher education institution was located. The former influence may be associated with age and maturity, since working class withdrawers tended to be older than entrants and withdrawers from the middle class.

The relatively greater dislike of the city or town may be attributable to a relationship between class, age and the student's home location. However, since no information was collected on whether students were studying from a home base or had moved from their homes to study, this can be no more than a tentative speculation.

Ethnicity

As with social class, the question about ethnicity was asked only in the mail surveys. Only 45 of the 1623 respondents did not answer the question. The vast majority (92 per cent) of respondents described themselves as white. For the purposes of comparison, the responses of the non-white students were collapsed into 'black' (N = 19), 'Asian' (N = 81) and 'other' (N = 20). The small numbers of non-white respondents meant that the findings could not be tested for statistical significance.[9]

Black withdrawers reported a much greater incidence of financial problems and various difficulties in relationships with others than did the other groups. Other differences between the groups lay in the supportiveness of staff and in library provision. Sub-analyses suggest that further exploration might be worthwhile in these areas to see if the relative dissatisfaction of black students with staff support (nine of the nineteen respondents mentioned this as having a moderate or considerable influence on their withdrawal) is a more general problem, since of the other groups only about one in four reported such a level of influence. That library provision was a source of difference seemed to lie with the black and 'other' groups, for whom one in four, rather than one in about fourteen, reported that this was a moderate or considerable influence on withdrawal.

Entry through Clearing

The 'Clearing' process, whose purpose is to enable students to find places in higher education once the results of the A-level examinations are known, requires students to make rapid decisions regarding courses and institutions if they have failed to gain the grades required by those institutions at which they already have conditional acceptances. The A-level results are published in August and enrolment into most institutions takes place at the beginning of October.

It might be expected that, because of the pressure of time, those students entering higher education through Clearing would be more likely to report that they had made the wrong choice of the field of study than those who met the entry criteria. Surprisingly, there is little evidence to indicate that this was the case, though there were occasional comments like

> I took up the course through clearing. It was a sudden change of direction from Law. After a year I knew I should have stuck with the Law, Accounting was not for me.
>
> (Accounting and Finance)

However, Appendix 4(d) reveals that there were a number of differences between withdrawers who had entered via Clearing and those who had not needed to use this route, and these are summarized in Factors 1, 5 and 6 where 'Clearing students' cited more frequently than their 'non-Clearing' peers the poor quality of the student experience, financial need and dissatisfaction with aspects of institutional provision as influences on their withdrawal. It is relatively easy to suggest why the issue of institutional provision appears more strongly in reports from 'Clearing students': these students will probably have had a fair idea of the type of programme that they were seeking, and may have found this during the Clearing process — but will perhaps have chosen the institution on the basis of a telephone conversation, only to have found that the reality of the institution was not as they had imagined. At the finer-grained analytical level 'Clearing students' cited more often, as influences on their withdrawal, computing provision, library provision, social facilities and specialist equipment as well as the failure of the institution to meet their expectations — however, with the exception of the last, the frequency of citation was relatively low. It could be that unhappiness with the student experience, as recorded in responses to a variety of items, may reflect a discrepancy between what these students had expected and what they actually experienced in an institution that was likely to have been lower down the reputational and resource range than the institution they had initially chosen.

Financial problems (a main influence on withdrawal) also played a greater part in the withdrawal of 'Clearing students', but it is difficult to attribute a reason for this difference. There is, for instance, no relationship between mode of entry into higher education and social class (which might have been a proxy for financial strength).

Academic Subject Category

The programmes of study were identified as falling into one of HEFCE's ASCs or into one of the three hybrid composites of mixed subjects (predominantly Social Science and Humanities-based, predominantly Science-based and mixed Social Science/Humanities and Science) as previously shown in Table 4.1.

There were statistically significant differences between the ASCs in respect of Factors 1, 2, 3 and 4. Bonferroni *post hoc* comparisons in respect of the factors highlighted where the main differences lay and are given in Appendix 4(a)(ii): the original data from which the *post hoc* comparisons were drawn are given in Appendix 4(a)(i).

At risk of over-simplifying, the (poor) quality of the student experience in ASCs 10 (Art, Design and Performing Arts) and 4 (Engineering and Technology) was particularly likely to have been an influence on withdrawal, and the inability to cope with the academic demand of the programme was likewise influential in ASCs 1 (Clinical and Pre-clinical subjects) and 4 (Engineering and Technology), though it has to be noted that the numbers in ASC 1 were small. 'Withdrawers' from ASCs 8 (Social Science) and 2 (Subjects and Professions Allied to Medicine) were relatively *unlikely* to cite the wrong choice of programme as influential, and those from ASC 6 (Mathematics, IT and Computing) were likewise unlikely to cite unhappiness with the social environment as influential.

Looking more finely at the comparisons, the perceived difficulty of Engineering and Technology and of Clinical and Pre-clinical subjects had much more influence on withdrawal than — at the other end of the scale — did Subjects and Professions Allied to Medicine, Humanities, Education, Art, Design and Performing Arts, Social Science and mixed Arts programmes.[10] Insufficient academic progress was particularly cited as an influence on withdrawal in Clinical and Pre-clinical subjects, Engineering and Technology, the Built Environment and mixed Science programmes, and appeared to be least influential in respect of Education and Subjects and Professions Allied to Medicine. Engineering and Technology was particularly noticeable for students reporting the influence of a lack of study skills, and Art, Design and the Performing Arts was particularly noticeable for the influence on withdrawal of programme organization and the quality of the teaching. Students from the Clinical and Pre-clinical and mixed Science programmes most frequently reported the influence of stress related to the programme.

As might be expected, these and other differences that were detected tended to relate to aspects of the programme of study and its delivery. The data in respect of variation between ASCs are complex, and here it has been possible to point to only a few of the more striking findings. Readers may wish to delve into the data presented in Appendix 4(a)(i) in order to explore inter-ASC differences in greater detail.

In general, the data suggest that the withdrawers from Science-based programmes tend to have struggled to cope with their subjects. It is difficult to go any further on this limited evidence, but the findings do hint at questions about the selection of students for such programmes, the approaches to teaching and learning that are employed and the general cultural ambience of the disciplinary area. At the other end of the disciplinary spectrum, the evidence presented here raises a question about the way in which programmes are implemented in the category of Art, Design and Performing Arts: could it be that the liberalism of approach not uncommon in that category is being perceived by some students as casual and unsupportive?

Programme type

Programme type was treated as a simple dichotomy (degree as opposed to sub-degree programme) for the purpose of analysis, the vast majority (85 per cent) of withdrawers coming from the former category. Notable differences between the two categories were few in number and not susceptible to easy interpretation. Those who withdrew from sub-degree programmes cited, more often than did their counterparts from degree programmes, their institution's provision of computing facilities and specialist equipment and also their programme's lack of relevance to their intended career.

Single or multiple subject programme

There is only one statistically significant difference of particular note between those students who took single-subject programmes and those who took multiple-subject programmes,[11] which does not admit of easy interpretation. Students who took single-subject programmes cited, as influential on their non-completion, the lack of academic progress to a greater extent than did those who took multiple-subject programmes, and other components of Factor 2 (inability to cope with programme demand) came close to meeting the significance criterion. This finding leads one to wonder whether, in general, single-subject programmes might be more academically demanding than multi-subject programmes — but this research provides no evidence either way.

Match of entry qualifications

There was only one difference of note between those students whose entry qualifications were a good match with the higher education programme they had studied and those for whom the match was partial or weak. Not surprisingly, this was in respect of having chosen the wrong field of study; those whose programmes were a partial or a weak match with their qualifications cited 'wrong choice' more often than did those whose match was good.

Institutional type

At the gross level of the six factors, there were significant differences between respondents from different types of institution on Factor 2 (inability to cope with the demands of the programme), with those from the pre-1992 universities least able to cope. At the finer level of the individual item (see Appendix 4(f) for details), the main differences between the influences on withdrawal from the three types of institution seem to centre on the choice of study programme. The wrong choice of field of study, lack of commitment and programme difficulty[12] were all more frequently cited as influences on withdrawal by respondents from pre-1992 universities than by those from the post-1992 universities and colleges.

A similar differentiation was apparent in two variables which are, for the body of students as a whole, relatively low in salience for withdrawal: homesickness and difficulty in making friends.

The seeking of advice about withdrawal

The mail questionnaire asked students whether they had sought advice prior to withdrawing and, if so, from whom. Sixty per cent had sought advice from somewhere inside their institution. Table 4.4 shows the extent to which various institution-related sources of advice were contacted (the percentages are of the total number of respondents and do not add to 60 because many students sought advice from more than a single source). In addition, 49 per cent of the students had sought advice from sources external to the institution, such as parents.

These results, with personal tutors and lecturers at the top of the list, indicate the abiding importance of the staff–student relationship at a time when, because of the pressure of numbers, the pastoral aspect of the academic's role has been under threat.

Table 4.4   Sources of institutional advice prior to withdrawal

Source of advice within institution	Percentage of respondents
Personal tutor	40.4
Lecturer	25.5
Other students	14.3
Careers officer	14.2
Counsellor	8.6
Welfare officer	4.8
Student union	4.2
Religious figure	0.7
Hall warden	0.1

Return to study

Of the 2151 respondents, 53 per cent indicated that they had already returned to study in higher education and a further 20 per cent indicated their intention to do so in the near future. These were combined into a group of 'returners' for the purposes of analysis, since these two groups were clearly different from those who had no plans to return. The original institution was favoured by 15 per cent of all respondents, whereas a different institution was favoured by 48 per cent. For those who responded to the question, there was a roughly even split between pursuing the same or a similar programme and a significantly different programme. Repetition of a year's worth of study would be undertaken by a similar number to those who expected to continue their studies without loss of time. The choice of the same or a new institution made little difference to the relative proportions repeating, or not repeating, a year's worth of study. However, there was a difference when the nature of the programme was related to the choice of institution. Of those choosing the same institution the ratio of those seeking to pursue the same or a similar programme to that opting for a significantly different programme was nearly 3:1. The corresponding ratio for those choosing a different institution was roughly 1:1. A 'flow chart' of these data is given in Figure 4.1.

Summary

Three main influences on withdrawal dominate the responses of the full-time and sandwich students. Roughly equal in frequency of citation were the wrong choice of the field of study and financial problems, with matters relating to the quality of the student experience a little further back. Analysis showed that the influences on withdrawal could be reduced to six factors:

- poor quality of the student experience;
- inability to cope with the demands of the programme;
- unhappiness with the social environment;
- wrong choice of programme;
- matters related to financial need; and
- dissatisfaction with aspects of institutional provision.

Younger students cited, more frequently than their older peers, the wrong choice of field of study and influences related to their unpreparedness for living away from home. In contrast, the older students found the demands of employment whilst studying a relatively more powerful influence on their departure.

When the data were 'cut' according to gender, men indicated more frequently than women that they were unhappy with aspects of their choice of field of study and that aspects of their personal finances had caused difficulty.

Figure 4.1 Full-time/sandwich students and their return to study after withdrawal or failure (those who had already returned and those intending to return are combined for the purposes of this analysis). The percentages relate to the original number of respondents, 2151. Numbers decline across the figure because of non-response and 'don't know' responses

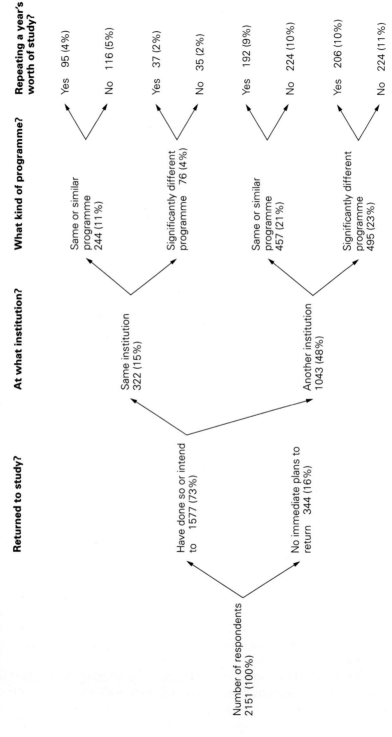

On the other hand, women expressed dissatisfaction with features of the social environment more frequently than men.

Working class students cited financial problems as influential on their departure more frequently than other students. These students were less likely to return to higher education at some time in the future. Students describing themselves as middle or upper class tended, to a greater extent than others, to admit that they had made wrong choice of field of study. It is likely that this finding correlates with youth and immaturity.

The patterns of influence on withdrawal differed from one Academic Subject Category to another. It seems probable that some of the differences relate to the cultures of the respective disciplines subsumed by the ASCs, but other factors such as entry calibre and age on entry seem likely to have exerted an effect.

Academics were the respondents' predominant source of advice regarding leaving. However, a fair number of respondents had received advice from members of their institution's student support services.

Over half of the respondents had returned to study within a year or so of departure and about a quarter indicated an intention to return. The returners were three times as likely to go to a different institution than to re-enrol at that from which they had withdrawn. If their return was to the same institution, they were much more likely to be going back to the same or a similar programme, but if to a different institution they were evenly divided as to whether they would be undertaking a similar or a significantly different programme.

Notes

1. More detail regarding the background of the respondents is given in Appendix 1.
2. It is not possible to give the proportion which had withdrawn during or at the end of the first year but HESA data for the institutions involved allows the inference that it was about two-thirds.
3. In this analysis the four-point scale was treated parametrically. The data are, strictly, ordinal — but a comparison of Spearman *rho* and Pearson *r* correlation matrices, and the six-factor solutions derived from them, showed a very high degree of similarity. Since factor scores were obtainable from SPSS only via the Pearson *r* matrix, this was used as input into the factor analysis reported here. Oblimin rotation offered no additional clarity.
4. Only the subject of study is noted against quotations (and in some cases even this has been generalized), since the type of programme and the type of institution could lead to the identification of particular institutions and, in a few cases, possibly of individuals.
5. For these comparisons the criterion was taken as $p < .01$, given the numbers involved. The significance of identified differences should be treated as indicative rather than definitive, given some uncertainty about the relationship between the sample and the population and because the same set of data was 'cut' in a number of different ways.

6. Men were asked if their partner's pregnancy was an influence on their withdrawal.
7. There is a hint in the data that responsibility in respect of dependants might tail off for students aged 35 and over, perhaps because of parental death.
8. Using the broad categories of (1) upper and middle class, (2) no particular class and (3) working class.
9. The relevant contingency table did not meet the criteria for use of the chi-square test (see Siegel and Castellan, 1988, p. 123).
10. There is, as Johnes and Taylor (1990a) pointed out, likely to be some differentiation between institutions on the basis of 'subject mix'.
11. Multiple-subject programmes include joint honours, major/minor and combined studies programmes. Both single-subject and multiple-subject programmes may or may not be modular in character.
12. Kahn and Hoyles (1997) have demonstrated that the demand of courses in Mathematics appears to have eased in recent years.

Chapter 5

'It's the economy, stupid':
Why Part-time Students Leave Early

Orientation

The structure of this chapter parallels that of Chapter 4. The chapter begins with a description of the background characteristics of the students. This is followed by an analysis of the influences on their departures which shows how different from those on full-time and sandwich students are the pressures on part-time students. Further analysis reveals six factors that, despite the differences between the two groups of students regarding the intensity of the influences on departure, exhibit considerable similarity with those from the analysis of data from the full-time and sandwich students; these factors are also elaborated in qualitative terms. A series of sub-group analyses then follows, but this is less extensive than that in Chapter 4 because of the much smaller number of students involved. Sources of advice for the potential leaver are indicated and comparison made with the situation for full-time and sandwich students. The flow of withdrawn students back into higher education is shown.

What were the backgrounds of the respondents?

The total number of part-time students who responded to the two mail surveys was 328, the vast majority of whom came from post-1992 universities. Very few came from pre-1992 universities. As Appendix 1 shows, about two-thirds of the respondents came from three Academic Subject Categories — Subjects and Professions Allied to Medicine, Business and Management, and Social Science. Compared with the full-time and sandwich respondents, a much higher proportion of the part-time respondents had been studying sub-degree programmes, probably reflecting the incidence of professional programmes in subjects allied to Medicine and in Business and Management. A greater proportion of part-time respondents than full-time and sandwich students had been studying single-subject programmes.

Women respondents outnumbered men by a ratio of 2:1 (in contrast to the 1:1 for the full-time and sandwich students), but the distribution of social class of the respondents was very similar to that for full-time and sandwich students. A large majority of the respondents was, as would be expected, aged

25 or more on enrolment on to their programmes. Almost all the students were white and almost all said that they did not have a disability.

Findings

The list of influences on non-completion acknowledged by the part-time respondents are headed by personal pressures that largely come from outside the educational system. The demands of employment whilst studying dominate the list, as is shown in Table 5.1. The contrast with the full-time and sandwich students is very marked apart from the relatively high acknowledgement given by all students to the influence of financial problems. Making allowance for significance of financial problems across all types of student, Table 5.1 can be summarized as indicating that, in general, part-time students who have withdrawn tend to cite personal pressures deriving from 'trying to deal with too many things', whereas their full-time and sandwich peers cite poor choice of study programme and dissatisfaction with 'the student experience'. The difference between the two groups is captured in the low correlation (Pearson *r*) between the two columns of Table 5.1, which is a mere 0.29 (and not statistically significant[1]).

The responses were subjected to principal components analysis with varimax rotation using the same approach employed in respect of the full-time and sandwich students.[2] The outcomes of this analysis are shown in Appendix 3(b): a six-factor solution accounted for 47.8 per cent of the variance. The six factors are as shown in Table 5.2.

The six factors bear a considerable similarity to those found for the full-time and sandwich respondents. Judging by the items that have dominant loadings on the factors, three are very similar indeed: dissatisfaction with aspects of institutional provision, wrong choice of programme and unhappiness with the extra-institutional environment. 'Poor quality of the student experience' contains the same main items in each case, but for the part-time students four additional items make the nature of the factor a little less sharply defined. Likewise, a core of items is common to the factor in which financial problems and the lack of personal support from family are to the fore — but the former loads much less heavily, and the latter much more heavily, in the case of the part-time students.

The most noticeable difference relates to the item 'demands of employment whilst studying'. For many full-time students these days, employment is an important but secondary aspect of their lives, the money earned being used to offset the expenses of being a student. For the typical part-time student, employment is a central necessity and the study programme is secondary but important. It is not surprising to find, therefore, that the demands of employment are — for part-time students — associated with stress, a workload that is too heavy and lack of commitment to the programme. After all, employment (which is usually full-time) and academic study can in their different ways be

Table 5.1   Influences on the decision to withdraw[1]

Variable	Percentage indicating moderate or considerable influence	
	PT	FT and SW
Demands of employment whilst studying	52	15
Needs of dependants	26	15
Workload too heavy	25	17
Financial problems	23	37
Programme organization	22	27
Inadequate staff support outside timetable	21	24
Timetabling did not suit	21	11
Teaching did not suit me	19	31
Quality of teaching	19	23
Lack of personal support from staff	17	24
Personal health problems	17	23
Stress related to the programme	16	22
Programme not what I expected	15	37
Lack of commitment to the programme	14	38
Class sizes too large	14	16
Emotional difficulties with others	13	23
Travel difficulties	13	15
Lack of personal support from family	12	12
Difficulty of the programme	10	21
Institutional library provision	10	8
Needed a break from education	9	28
Taking up employment*	8	10
Programme not relevant to my career	8	23
Insufficient academic progress	8	30
Chose wrong field of study	7	39
Institution not what I expected	7	19
Institutional computing facilities	7	9
Pregnancy (self or partner's)*	7	6
Lack of study skills	6	17
Bereavement of someone close*	6	6
Lack of personal support from students	5	15
Institutional provision of specialist equipment	3	7
Fear of crime	2	10
Difficulty in making friends	2	9
Institutional provision of social facilities	2	9
Accommodation problems	2	18
Dislike of city/town	1	15
Problems with drugs/alcohol	1	7
Homesickness	0	11

1. Cited by 328 part-time students, compared with those influences cited by 2151 full-time and sandwich students. Valid numbers per item for the part-time students are 328, with the exception of the three asterisked items which were only included in the 1995–96 mail survey and attracted 196 responses in each case. The corresponding numbers for the full-time and sandwich students can be found in Table 4.2.

highly demanding activities. Given the primacy of the former, it is not surprising that Table 5.1 shows that the demands of employment are by far the most heavily cited influence on withdrawal. As Bill Clinton was wont to remind himself, 'It's the economy, stupid!' — but here 'the economy' is used in at least a trivalent sense to reflect the demands of the workplace, the pressure of

Table 5.2   Labels for the six factors

Factor no.	% variance	Label
1	17.3	Poor quality of the student experience
2	8.1	Pressure of work (academic and employment)
3	7.3	Unhappiness with the extra-institutional environment
4	5.6	Problems with relationships and finance
5	4.9	Dissatisfaction with aspects of institutional provision
6	4.6	Wrong choice of programme

dependants on the student's time-budget and to some extent the impact of study on personal finances.

As was noted in respect of the similar analysis reported in Chapter 4, care has to be taken not to confuse the size of the factor with its importance. Table 5.1 shows that the demands of employment whilst studying are at least twice as likely to be cited as an influence on withdrawal than any other influence, yet this item appears only in Factor 2.

Relatively few additional comments were made by part-time students when they responded to the questionnaire and so it is not possible to provide the richness of quotation that was possible in the previous chapter. All that will be done here is to summarize the factors as shown in Table 5.2 and to give the occasional illustrative comment where it is available and appropriate.

Factor 1: Poor quality of the student experience

This factor sweeps up lack of support from staff, quality of the teaching, the organization of the programme and the size of classes. Comments relevant to these items included the following:

> Part time students are treated like full time students, little sympathy or flexibility prevailed. Some tutors treated part time students like children.
>
> (Law)

> Not enough feedback on projects completed — no indication when asked for on shortcomings of projects.
>
> (Business)

The lack of personal support from students comes into this factor, perhaps because for many part-time students the only peer contact they have is during the programme — and one might infer a desire for this aspect of their experience to be strengthened, perhaps via mutual-support groups. Age difference was noted by one respondent as a problem:

> I was one of the oldest in the class (35+) and although I do not have problems getting on with or relating to younger people — I felt there was definitely a 'gap'.
>
> (Business)

Insufficiency of academic progress may be related causally to dissatisfaction with the general student experience. It would appear that these students are tending to see the process of selecting a programme and an institution as part of the general student experience. One student wrote:

> Prior to enrolment we spoke to the course tutor on two occasions and he assured my colleagues and I that the course was very well suited to our requirements, but once the course started it was blatantly obvious this was not the case. It is obvious to me that I should not have been told by [institution] that the course was suitable. On reflection it seems that they were only interested in getting people to enrol on the course rather than their academic suitability.
> (Business)

Factor 2: Pressure of work (academic and employment)

This factor subsumes the twin pressures of employment and academic work, which may account for the correlation with difficulties students find regarding the timetabling of the programme. Stress would seem to be a causally related outcome, as — perhaps — does lack of commitment to the programme (which also loads slightly more strongly on Factor 6).

As one student put it (with some lack of precision, but the meaning is fairly clear nevertheless):

> My commitment to my employment made it extremely difficult to arrive to our classes on time or miss classes and left little time for studying.
> (Business)

Factor 3: Unhappiness with the extra-institutional environment

This factor brings together dislike of the city or town, fear of crime, homesickness and problems with accommodation. Given that the respondents are part-time students, this factor is difficult to interpret, for it would be expected that homesickness and problems with accommodation would have little part to play in such students' decisions regarding continuation of study. However, the other two items have a more obvious bearing on students who may be leaving their institutions as late as 9pm and worry about being attacked or finding that their cars have been vandalized.

Factor 4: Problems with relationships and finance

The dominant items in this factor are concerned with relationships — lack of support from family, emotional difficulties with others and needs of dependants. With financial problems loading on to this factor, the factor might equally have been labelled 'domestically related stress'.

However, not all financial difficulties were laid by students at their own door. Mention was made by a few of the lack of financial or time support from the employer:

> My employers did not support my application to study — by giving adequate time and money.
>
> (Health Studies)

> There was lack of support from my employer. It was bad enough spending most evenings and weekends studying during my HNC without contemplating another three years of the same.
>
> (Management)

Factor 5: Dissatisfaction with aspects of institutional provision

This factor, which subsumes the provision of library, computing, specialist equipment and social facilities, is fairly sharply defined but — as Table 5.1 clearly shows — is of minimal importance. These are items that contribute little to individuals' decisions to withdraw from higher education.

Factor 6: Wrong choice of programme

It would be expected that wrong choice of field of study and the programme's perceived lack of relevance to the student's career would appear in the same factor. Equally, it is unsurprising to find programmes not as expected and lack of commitment loading on to the same factor. None of these items contributes particularly strongly to student withdrawal, as Table 5.1 shows — but a measure of surprise must exist that some students who are generally not under time-pressure to enrol, and who are likely to be limited in regard to the institutions they can consider, nevertheless make choices which they later come to regret.

Exploratory analyses

The relatively limited number of responses, coupled with the spread of substantial part-time work across a small number of Academic Subject Categories in post-1992 universities and colleges, allowed fewer exploratory analyses to be conducted than was possible for the full-time and sandwich students. Details of the exploratory analyses can be found in some of the tables in Appendix 4.

Age

On the six factor scores, there were no significant differences between students who were 25 and above compared with their under 25 peers. At a finer level of analysis, the evidence shows that the younger group was more likely to cite, as an influence on their withdrawal, stress related to the programme.

Gender

There were no significant differences between male and female students in respect of their scores on the six factors. A more close-grained examination of the data suggests that there are two areas — needs of dependants and the ability to cope with the programme — in which gender-related differences may exist. Not surprisingly, the needs of dependants were cited more often by female than male withdrawers. Less susceptible of explanation is the finding that male withdrawers cited the difficulty of the programme to a greater extent than did women. This would seem to relate to a greater tendency of men to say that lack of academic progress was influential on their departure.

Social class

There are few differences discernible with reference to self-reported social class (stratified, it will be recalled, into working class, 'no particular class' and middle/upper class). There is a difference between the three groups in respect of Factor 1, where middle/upper class respondents were significantly less happy with the quality of the student experience than the other groups of respondents. Students of 'no particular class' tended to have been least dissatisfied in this respect. Fine-grained analysis suggested that the foci of the difference were the quality of the teaching and programme organization.

The other influence which, at the fine-grained level, showed a significant difference between the three categories of class is that of emotional difficulties with others, with middle/upper class respondents citing this influence to a lesser extent than the other two categories. The quantitative data do not provide an explanation for this difference, but it is possible to speculate on the possibility of an 'Educating Rita' syndrome. Those familiar with the film will recall the emotional stresses in the fictitious working class Rita's life which followed her enrolment on an Open University course.

Academic Subject Category

As noted in the first section of this chapter, the bulk of the respondents came from ASCs 2 (Subjects and Professions Allied to Medicine), 7 (Business and Management) and 8 (Social Science), and from the post-1992 universities. Ignoring differences in institutional type, there were few differences of any note between respondents from the three different ASCs.[3] Factors 3 (unhappiness with the extra-institutional environment) and 5 (dissatisfaction with aspects of institutional provision) did differentiate between the groups, respondents from Social Science scoring relatively highly in each case. The first of the differences can probably be discounted for practical purposes since it encompasses four main items for which the citation level is very low. The data relating to Factor 5 are probably of greater practical significance as the fine-grained analysis shows that students from Social Science stood out in indicating that deficiencies in library and computing provision had been influential on their withdrawal. The findings hint at questions which, to begin with, would need to be underpinned by data from persisting students: is there inequity in the funding of different subject disciplines and, if so, is it Social Science that appears to require a higher provision of learning resource, perhaps to a level greater than the norm for 'classroom-based' disciplines?

Level of programme

There was a significant difference between withdrawers from sub-degree programmes and those from degree-level programmes as far as Factor 4 (finance and personal relationships) was concerned, the latter evidencing the stronger influence on withdrawal. The finer-grained data offer little by way of elaboration. Financial problems were cited as a stronger influence on withdrawal from degree than from sub-degree programmes; the difference is statistically significant. This difference may well be connected with the greater length of time to achieve a degree than, say, a Higher National Certificate, and hence the greater outlay on fees and other expenses, and it seems possible that other influences, such as the needs of dependants and the demands of employment, are combining to induce in the students a qualitative judgement against a composite (and perhaps unarticulated) 'value for money and effort' criterion.

Students on degree programmes cited, more often than did their counterparts on sub-degree programmes, the influence of health problems on their withdrawal. One reason for this may lie in the greater duration of part-time degrees, which necessarily increases the chance that a student will withdraw on health-related grounds at some time during such a programme.

Single- or multiple-subject programme

It made almost no difference whether the respondent had followed a single-subject or a multi-subject degree programme. The single statistically significant difference of note related to the difficulty of the programme, where the difficulty of a multi-subject programme seems to have been more influential on withdrawal than that of a single-subject programme. This finding runs counter to that from the full-time and sandwich students, though why a difference should exist is obscure.

The seeking of advice from within the institution before leaving

The availability of advice from institutional staff is of increasing importance as institutions develop their quasi-contractual relationships with students (through charters and the like). For students who attend an institution on only one or two evenings a week the availability of support services may be limited.

A minority of the students sought advice from within the institution before leaving. The main sources of advice were academic staff, either lecturers or personal tutors; only one-eighth of those who sought advice from within the institution asked both a lecturer and their personal tutor for it. The third most frequent source of advice was other students. Noticeably little used were other support staff within the institutions, such as counsellors and welfare officers (Table 5.3). This may be related to the daytime hours normally worked by such staff.

Table 5.3   Part-time students' sources of advice regarding leaving (some students cited more than a single source of advice)

Source of advice	Number of respondents	Percentage of the total number of respondents (328)
Lecturer	66	20.1
Personal tutor	55	16.8
Other students	20	6.1
Welfare officer	6	1.8
Careers officer	4	1.2
Counsellor	3	0.9
Students' Union	1	0.3
Religious figure	0	0.0
Other, unspecified	13	4.0

The data in Table 5.3 do hint at the restricted availability of institutional support personnel (other than lecturing staff) for students whose attendance is predominantly in the evenings. An institutional commitment to the quality of the student experience (in its broadest sense) does require that part-time students are not treated inequitably in the provision of support services.

Return to study

More than half of the respondents had returned to study approximately a year after they had withdrawn from study. Figure 5.1 shows the 'flow' of the respondents either back into higher education or out of the system. The 're-turners' were roughly evenly split between the same and another institution, which may reflect the density of opportunities in the north-west of England in which perhaps ten institutions are within relatively easy reach of the Liverpool–Manchester corridor (particularly by car). The situation is very likely to be different where there is a lower concentration of institutions, such as — say — in Lincolnshire or Cornwall.

Figure 5.1 The 'flow' of part-time students back into study

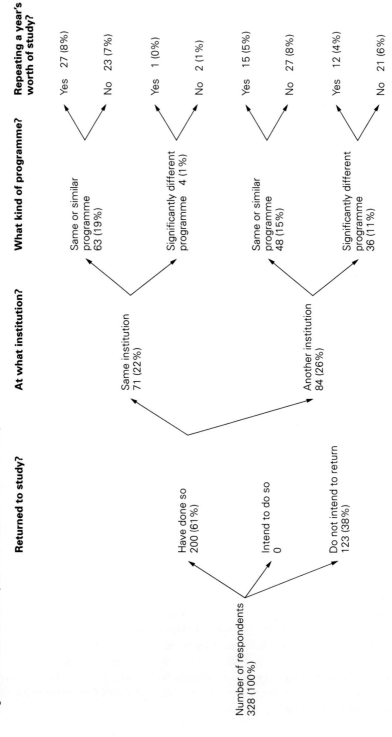

Where students had returned to the same institution, the vast majority had returned to the same or a similar programme, and about half of these students were repeating a year's worth of study. In contrast, where they had switched to another institution the chances were only slightly greater than evens that they were following the same or a similar programme, and only a minority were repeating a year's worth of study.

Summary

The bulk of responses from students came from post-1992 universities, pre-1992 universities and colleges being thinly represented in the distribution of responses.

For the part-time students who responded to the surveys, the demands of employment were the most cited influence on withdrawal and were cited twice as often as the needs of dependants, the magnitude of the workload and financial problems. Despite the marked differences in causality compared with that of the full-time and sandwich students, there was considerable similarity in the six factors that were thrown up by analysis, which were

- poor quality of the student experience;
- pressure of work (academic and employment);
- unhappiness with the extra-institutional environment;
- problems with relationships and finance;
- dissatisfaction with aspects of institutional provision; and
- wrong choice of programme.

Exploratory analyses of the comparatively small number of responses showed few differences of significance between sub-groups of part-time students.

Academic staff were predominant in the provision of advice prior to students' leaving. Very few students had sought advice from members of institutional student support services.

The majority of withdrawers had returned to study a year or so after they had departed. This group divided roughly equally between return to the same institution (in which case almost all had returned to the same academic programme) and to a different institution (where there was a near even split between return to a similar programme or a significantly different programme).

Notes

1. The criterion for statistical significance in this chapter is taken as $p < .05$, in recognition of the smaller numbers compared with those of Chapter 4. The same caution regarding the interpretation of statistical significance applies.
2. See note 3 to Chapter 4.
3. Particular caution has to be taken when interpreting these data since the other ASCs were eliminated from consideration because the numbers of students from them were too low for statistical comparisons.

Chapter 6

The Cost to the Taxpayer

Orientation

This chapter is concerned with the cost to public finances of full-time and sandwich students' non-completion in English institutions. In 1994–95 this cost had three components — core funding, tuition fees and student maintenance awards — in respect of which a number of technical assumptions had to be made. Profiles of cost are built up on the basis of different conceptions of non-completion and a best estimate of the cost to the public purse is derived.

What is, and what is not, being estimated

In this chapter the estimates that are being made regarding the direct cost to the public purse for the academic year 1994–95 of full-time and sandwich students' non-completion exclude teacher education since this was (and still is) financed through a separate organization, the Teacher Training Agency. The choice of the year 1994–95 allowed reasonably reliable estimates to be made of the effects of return to study, since empirical data had been gathered regarding the proportion of withdrawers who had returned to study by the autumn of 1996.[1]

The flexibility with which part-time students participate in higher education means that it is more difficult to make comparable estimates in respect of their non-completion, and hence these have not been attempted here. This is less of a weakness than it might seem since in 1994–95 part-time students constituted in number only about one-third of that of their full-time and sandwich peers,[2] their fees are normally not paid from public funds and they were not eligible for maintenance awards when those were available. The cost to public finances of part-time students is, in effect, limited to the provision of 'core funding' for the place in the higher education institution.

The costs to other stakeholders are not considered here and may be considerable: for example, some students have to repay loans taken out in respect of programmes from which they have withdrawn. Further, Johnes and Taylor (1991) found — unsurprisingly — that failure to complete a degree course led to persistently lower earnings than graduation, and Blundell et al. (1997) found that those who entered higher education but failed to obtain any qualification received lower wages than those who did not enter higher education at all.[3]

The components of cost to public finances

The direct cost to public finances is associated with three components: HEFCE core funding for places, the tuition fees paid to the institution and the maintenance awards paid to students for the period prior to withdrawal and not repaid to the providing local education authority (LEA). Non-completion is not necessarily 'wastage' and the estimate of direct cost has to be offset in the light of two considerations: first, the fact that some students will pick up their studies after a period out of higher education and, second, the student may have benefited even though he or she may have failed to complete the full programme for which he or she was enrolled. In respect of the latter, some will have gained intermediate qualifications, such as a Certificate or Diploma of Higher Education,[4] and others will have gained credits which they can subsequently 'cash in' against subsequent studies. Still others will have benefited from their time in higher education, even if they have gained few or no formal credentials as a result.

Estimating the cost to public finances

Core funding

In order to trigger the release of the HEFCE core funding, the student has to complete the academic year (but not necessarily have passed the end-of-year examinations), which for student-related purposes can — for most institutions — be taken as ending in the middle of July.[5] In practice, it is unlikely that funding will have been withheld for a student who was officially in attendance at the beginning of June, and so a cut-off date of 31 May has been used in the estimation that follows.

The release of HEFCE funding is based on institutional Higher Education Student Enrolment Survey (HESES) returns on 1 December each year, adjusted for late entrants and estimated withdrawal rates. The HESES data would therefore not comprise a well-grounded basis for the estimation of the actual cost to the public purse of non-completion. The HESA data for 1994–95 is acknowledged to have some weaknesses, but has been taken as the best available and has been used as the starting-point for the estimates which follow.[6]

The costs of core funding (Average Unit of Council Funding (AUCF)) for each ASC were taken from HEFCE (1995) and are listed in Table 6.1.

The following assumptions have been made regarding the relationship between time of withdrawal and cost. If the student withdrew

- by 31 May, then cost has been taken as zero because release of funding is not triggered;[7] and
- after 31 May, then the full funding for the place has been assumed to have been released.

Table 6.1   AUCFs and fee bands for ASCs 1 to 10 and for combined programmes spanning ASCs

ASC	AUCF £	Fee band	Comments
1	5947	2/3	Weighted mean of the AUCFs for the component subjects in this ASC. Fee assumed to split 40/60 for Pre-clinical (Band 2)/Clinical subjects (Band 3): £2320 used throughout the calculations.[1]
2	2565	1/2	Assumed to split 50/50 between Bands 1, 2.
3	2925	2	
4	3351	2	
5	2208	2	
6	2380	1/2	Assumed to split 10/90 between Bands 1, 2.
7	1865	1	
8	1834	1	
9	2018	1	
10	2200	2	
Combined	2100	Assumed 1	An assumed mean AUCF.

1. Fee arrangements vary in practice between institutions, with some making a sharper distinction between Pre-clinical and Clinical subjects than others.

Table 6.2   The fees applicable in 1994–95, by subject band

Band	Fee £
1	750
2	1600
3	2800

Tuition fees

Institutions receive tuition fees in three equal tranches, according to actual student enrolments on 15 November, 15 February and 31 May each year. If a student withdraws before one of these dates, then the fee for the preceding period is not paid to the institution.

Subjects were allocated to one of three bands in 1994–95 on the basis of the amount of practical work involved. Medicine and Dentistry, for example, appeared in Band 3, Art and Design, Engineering and Science in Band 2 and subjects held not to require practical facilities in Band 1. The fees that were applicable to the three subject bands are given in Table 6.2.

The following assumptions have been made regarding the relationship between time of withdrawal and cost. If the student withdrew

- by 15 November, then cost has been taken as zero because no fees are payable;
- between 16 November and 15 February, then cost has been taken as one-third of the fee;
- between 16 February and 31 May, then cost has been taken as two-thirds of the fee; and
- after 31 May, then cost has been taken as the full fee.

Maintenance awards

Until 1998 students were entitled to a means-tested maintenance award through the relevant LEA, whose intention was to contribute to the student's living and studying expenses. A student withdrawing during an academic year was expected to repay to the LEA the maintenance award in full if his or her entitlement to any further maintenance award were not to be compromised.

The Statistics Branch of the Department for Education and Employment provided information that the mean maintenance award for 1994–95 was £1515 (excluding teacher training programmes).

The following assumptions have been made regarding the relationship between time of withdrawal and cost. If the student withdrew

- before 31 October, then it has been assumed that no maintenance award cost was incurred;
- between 31 October and 31 January, it has been assumed that 50 per cent of students will not have returned their awards; and
- after 31 January, it has been assumed that no students will have returned their awards.

This third component is the most problematic as guesstimates have had to be made regarding the return of awards by non-completing students.

The profile of withdrawal across the academic year

From the HESA national file for 1994–95 data were extracted about the numbers of withdrawals by Academic Subject Category. These enabled the construction of a profile of withdrawals for each fortnight through the year.[8] The withdrawal profile was subdivided into two parts, first-year withdrawals and withdrawals from the beginning of the second year of study, on the grounds that the pattern of first-year withdrawal tends to differ from that of subsequent years.[9] The assumption has been made that the distribution of withdrawals is consistent across ASCs and (with the exception of the first year) across years. This is an approximation that could be refined with reference to detailed data but, given the uncertainty inherent in other aspects of the estimation of costs, it was decided that there was little point in straining at the gnat of precision in this component.

Table 6.3 Specimen example estimating the cost of non-completion for full-time and sandwich students in ASC 4 for the year 1994–95

Source of cost	Withdrawal period	Year 1 (N withdrawers = 3316) Proportion of withdrawers	Subsequent years (N withdrawers = 1229) Proportion of withdrawers	Year 1 £k	Subsequent years £k	Total £k
Core funding	By 31 May	0.770	0.681	0	0	
	After 31 May	0.230	0.319	2556	1314	3870
Tuition fees	By 15 November	0.218	0.211	0	0	
	16 Nov to 15 Feb	0.358	0.275	633	180	
	16 Feb to 31 May	0.194	0.195	687	256	
	After 31 May	0.230	0.319	1220	627	3603
Maintenance	By 31 October	0.167	0.177	0	0	
	1 Nov to 31 Jan	0.346	0.255	869	237	
	After 31 January	0.487	0.568	2447	1058	4611
Overall total						12,084

Method of calculating the estimate

The data from the preceding sections was used in the estimation of the cost of non-completion according to the example for ASC 4 which is given in Table 6.3. Each component of the cost was calculated according to the following formula:

$$\text{Cost} = p_1 \times N \times p_2 \times r$$

where p_1 is the proportion of the student body leaving during the stated period;

       N is the number of students;

       p_2 is the proportion of the cost estimated to have been paid from public sources (see earlier sections); and

       r is the rate of funding (core funding, fee, maintenance) that applies (again, see earlier sections).

According to HESA data, there were 4545 withdrawals (voluntary and involuntary) from English institutions[10] in ASC 4 (Engineering and Technology), 3316 in Year 1 and a total of 1229 in subsequent years.[11]

At this stage it is assumed that there is no cost of withdrawal for those years which the student may have completed successfully. Later, consideration is given to the opposite — and most sceptical — assumption that failure to complete a course of study implies a benefit-less cost to the public purse. Further, no consideration has been given at this stage to the fact that a considerable proportion of 'non-completers' go on to complete a programme of study after a period of intercalation. This issue, too, is addressed below.

The withdrawal rates of sandwich students *during the sandwich placement* are extremely low, and the costs associated with this are regarded as negligible in the context of this analysis.

The analysis presented below suffers from uncertainty regarding the scale of inter-year withdrawal as some students who are not coded in HESA returns may simply not return. An estimate of the costs of unacknowledged inter-year withdrawal has been deferred until later in this chapter.

The overall picture

The overall picture of cost is built up in three stages. The first is based on HESA data and makes no allowance for subsequent return to study. The second is also based on HESA data but takes return to study into account. The third develops the second stage further by taking into account the likelihood that the HESA data underestimate the true picture of withdrawal.

Table 6.4   The estimated overall cost of non-completion by ASC

	Overall cost £m	
ASC	Assuming that successful completion of a year implies no waste of public finances	Assuming that all of the time a non-completing student is a waste of public finances
1	0.7	2.9
2	2.6	5.9
3	10.3	20.3
4	12.1	22.6
5	3.1	6.9
6	8.7	16.6
7	8.9	16.4
8	5.4	10.2
9	5.4	10.9
10	6.1	12.2
Combined subjects	8.6	15.5
Overall	71.9	140.4

Stage 1: HESA data, no allowance for subsequent return to study

Table 6.4 summarizes the calculations of cost for each of the ASCs 1 to 10 and for those students who were undertaking combined programmes that spanned more than a single ASC. For combined programmes the mean cost of a funded place was estimated to be £2100, on the assumption that a relatively small proportion of the studies will have fallen into the fairly costly areas of provision (such as Science and Engineering).[12] Some students are likely to have been required, because of earlier withdrawal or failure, to fund themselves in 1994–95, but no information was available regarding the scale of this. The figures in Table 6.4 are therefore likely to be a slight overestimate as they need to be discounted to include only the core funding involved.

Table 6.4 also presents a 'worst case' picture — i.e. if all of a student's time in higher education up to the point of withdrawal or failure is regarded as wasted.

In the second column of Table 6.4 the inbuilt assumption is that years of study that have been completed successfully (i.e. the student has been permitted to continue into successive year(s) of his or her programme) are an appropriate return for the public finance that has been invested. If, however, the view is taken that this is not justified (for example, because a student reading for an MEng has decided to withdraw during the third year of the programme, having completed two years successfully), then the costs of non-completion have to be considered from a different perspective. The view might be taken that the cost to the public purse of the withdrawn engineer is the total of the investment in his or her education in Engineering, on the grounds that that was what he or she was being supported to do and that he or she had not 'delivered' on that investment.[13] Column 3 in Table 6.4 is based on the assumption that no economic benefit has accrued in respect of all of the time spent in higher education prior to departure. It therefore represents an 'upper boundary' to the cost to public finances of non-completion.

The best estimate of the costs of non-completion (not allowing for re-entry into higher education) probably lies very much closer to that of column 2 in Table 6.4 than that of column 3, on the grounds that many students who have successfully completed one or more full years of study will have gained credits or sufficient evidence for them to re-enter higher education without having to start again from scratch. A liberal humanist might wish to argue that, even if a student has nothing concrete to show for the time spent in higher education, he or she will often have gained in knowledge and skills that are of use in the world outside higher education.

The estimates of cost in Table 6.4 are in one important respect over-estimates because a substantial proportion of 'non-completers' return to study without the need to re-cover a year of study. Evidence collected from six institutions in the north-west of England showed that about three-quarters of respondents had either returned to study by the time of the survey or were thinking of returning in the near future. Only about a quarter did not foresee a return to higher education. If the proportion of actual and intending 'returners' can be taken as an estimate of the national picture, then those who return to study without any loss of progression in their studies should not in any respect be construed as a benefit-less cost to the public purse: data reported in Chapter 4 suggest that very nearly 40 per cent of withdrawers may fall into this category.[14] On the assumption that the distribution of such students is consistent across the ASCs,[15] this would suggest that the estimated overall cost to the public purse, as expressed in columns 2 and 3 of Table 6.4, ought to be scaled down to around £43m and £85m, respectively.

Stage 2: HESA data, but allowing for subsequent return to study

Of the respondents, just over one-third were repeating, or would have to repeat, a year of study. Such students take up a funded place in a higher education institution but are unlikely to be given support in terms of fees and maintenance. Taking this into account, making the assumptions that the proportion of 'repeaters' would be the same across the country and that the costs relate to the ASC which they had left,[16] and again making the assumption that the repetition of a year's worth of study is spread in the same proportion across ASCs, the overall costs shown in column 2 of Table 6.4 have to be amended to £69m. Column 3 is affected more substantially, since the assumption of 'total wastage' does not apply when students re-enter higher education and the bulk of them are successful. The net effect of all the 'modified total wastage' assumptions is that the cost to public finances is estimated at £89m — about 2.9 per cent of the total expenditure. In the light of the considerations laid out earlier, the best estimate of the costs of non-completion, allowing for the effects of return to study, is around £69m (which represents about 2.3 per cent of the total expenditure).

Stage 3: Assuming HESA data are underestimates, and allowing for return to study

Evidence collected from the six institutions in the north-west of England suggested that the number of unacknowledged inter-year withdrawers is about the same as the number of students who are recorded in the HESA data as having withdrawn. If this is the case, and the rough assumption is made that about half of the inter-year withdrawals result from academic failure,[17] then the figures in Table 6.4 become larger. Making the allowances for returning students with and without the need to repeat a year of study (as above), the best estimate of non-completion now becomes around £91.5m (Table 6.5) whereas the upper boundary estimate simply doubles to around £178m. Of the £91.5m estimate about £17m is attributable to the cost of tuition fees, £34m to the maintenance award and £41m to core funding.

Table 6.5 *The 'best estimate' of costs to the public purse, assuming that HESA data for 1994–95 understated the level of non-completion*

ASC	Overall cost £m
1	1.1
2	3.4
3	13.3
4	16.1
5	3.8
6	10.9
7	11.0
8	6.7
9	6.8
10	7.4
Combined subjects	11.0
Overall	*91.5*

Using the same basis for calculating the cost of educating all the full-time/sandwich students, the total cost of education in each ASC was determined and the ratios of the best estimates of costs of non-completion to the total ASC costs were determined (Table 6.6).

Table 6.6 shows that the percentage cost is not high (even though the actual cost runs into tens of millions of pounds)[18] and that it varies with ASC, with ASC 1 being particularly low in this respect. The pattern will not be unfamiliar to many in the system who are all too aware of the greater tendency for students in ASC 1 to complete and ASCs 4 and 6 not to complete their studies.[19] Given that the basis of calculation is consistent across all of the estimates

Table 6.6   Costs of non-completion expressed as percentages of the total cost of educational provision

ASC	'Best estimate' cost as % of total, using HESA data	'Best estimate' cost as % of total, assuming HESA data understates non-completion
1	0.6	0.7
2	2.1	2.7
3	2.0	2.7
4	3.0	3.9
5	2.5	3.4
6	3.2	4.3
7	2.6	3.5
8	1.8	2.3
9	1.7	2.3
10	2.1	2.7
Combined	2.6	3.4
All	*2.3*	*3.0*

of cost, it is likely that, if other approaches were used, the proportionalities would come out much the same. A benchmarking exercise such as this could provide a stimulus for institutions (which can replicate the calculation on an institution-specific level) to examine their practices and to see whether any reduction in the percentage cost of non-completion might be possible.

In these estimations no distinction has been drawn between academic failure and withdrawal; in fact, 19.1 per cent of the national record of withdrawing students are listed as having left as a result of failure. However, perhaps half of the inter-year withdrawals are attributable to failure, and therefore — if inter-year withdrawals are roughly similar in number to the withdrawals captured in the HESA record — the proportion of failure is likely to be around 35 per cent. On these assumptions, the costs of failure are likely to be of the order of £32m out of the 'best estimate' of £91.5m.[20]

Conclusions

The most likely estimate of the cost of full-time and sandwich undergraduate non-completion in the year 1994–95, taking into account students returning and perhaps repeating a year of study, is approximately £91m, which represents about 3 per cent of the total expenditure. This figure acknowledges that students who have completed the preceding year(s) of study have justified the investment in them for those years, and makes allowance for a probable understatement of non-completion in the HESA record. Had the funding system for students been that operational in the United Kingdom from 1998, then about half of the tuition fee expenditure, and all of the maintenance award expenditure, would not have been paid from public funds. This would leave the cost to the taxpayer of non-completion at somewhere in the region of £50m.[21]

If the most sceptical view is taken regarding non-completion in 1994–95 (i.e. that non-completion without subsequent return and/or repetition of a year's worth of study is a total waste of the public resources invested), then the estimate of cost to the taxpayer is about £178m, or 5.8 per cent of the total expenditure.

The cost attributable to academic failure appears to be about 35 per cent of the cost of non-completion.

A variation was noted between ASCs in the ratio of costs of non-completion to total costs. This implicitly raises questions as to why this should have been the case, and the method of approach has potential for institutional benchmarking against these national normative data.

The tracking of unacknowledged withdrawers is a much more complex exercise than could be undertaken in this study as it would involve a careful matching of student records in HESA's database. Students withdrawing from an institution may not be 'withdrawers' from the perspective of the higher education system as a whole. A pilot study from the system-level perspective has been conducted by HEFCE in which, because students in the United Kingdom do not have to supply a unique identifier (such as a Social Security number), matches had to be made by combining data from a number of fields.[22] This has been followed by a substantial study across English higher education in which the flow of students has been mapped for individual institutions and for the sector as a whole.[23]

Postscript

As this book was going to press Dobson and Sharma (1998) reported on their investigation of the cost of failure in Australian bachelor's degree education in 1996. Their calculations were based on failure in study units (broadly equivalent to modules), and covered some 437,000 Australian students (338,000 full-time equivalent students). The overall failure rate was calculated to be 11 per cent, but this overall figure masks considerable variation

- in different subject areas, where the extremes were in Mathematics (21 per cent) and in Medicine and other clinical subjects (2 per cent);
- between men and women, where the failure rate of the former averaged out at five percentage points higher than that of the latter (14 per cent against 9 per cent); and
- between modes of study, where there was a gradation of failure rate (full-time students 10, part-time students 13, and external [distance learning] students 17 per cent, respectively).

Dobson and Sharma estimated the public cost of failure to be $Aus269m (around £100m at the 1998 exchange rate), and the cost to individuals and private sponsors to be $Aus91m (£33m).

However, care needs to be taken when comparing Dobson and Sharma's figures with those presented in this chapter, since — as the authors are aware — failure in study units is not the same as non-completion. As in the United Kingdom, compensation may be applied in the case of failures in particular units, or a failure may be condoned for personal reasons such as illness. Students may also retake failed units and go on to complete their degress successfully, without loss of time.

Dobson and Sharma's work shows the power of the Australian higher education system's database, and implicitly its capacity to use the success (or failure) rate per study unit as a performance indicator: a more explicit demonstration of this capacity is given in Dobson et al., 1996. The potential of the unit non-completion rate (amongst others) is discussed, with reference to English higher education, in the next chapter.

Notes

1. Some had picked up their studies without any loss of time, whereas others were having to repeat a year's worth of study (see Chapter 4).
2. See HESA (1996, pp. 98, 106).
3. This runs counter to some earlier evidence from the Netherlands (Hartog, 1983).
4. It should be noted that some students are enrolled (for personal economic and/or institutional reasons) for the highest qualification for which they are eligible, even though their real intention is to aim for a lower level of award.
5. It should be noted that institutions incur costs when students fail to complete their year of study. Students who do not stay in the institution until the end of the academic year are not eligible for core funding from HEFCE, yet the institutions have to bear the costs of recruiting, enrolling and teaching them for the period before they withdraw.
6. The improvement in the quality of HESA data since 1994–95 will allow, for subsequent years, cross-checking of the accuracy of HESES estimations of student withdrawals and more accurate estimations of the cost of non-completion to be made.
7. Although, as noted earlier, institutions will have incurred costs as well.
8. This profile was based on full-time and sandwich 'Home' students in all institutions teaching undergraduates, with the exception of Oxford, Cambridge and the Open Universities and one other university which had submitted to HESA data that were manifestly in gross error. The profile will vary with institution since institutions low in the reputational range may lose students to those that are higher. This could account for the first year non-completion rate of 77 per cent found by Thomas et al. (1996) from an institution that was probably towards the lower end of the range against an English norm of about two-thirds. In these calculations, the average profile across all English institutions has been used.
9. The profiles for the withdrawal of first-year and other students can be found in Yorke et al. (1997b, Appendix 4).
10. Excluding the Universities of Oxford and Cambridge and the Open University.
11. Including three students for whom the year of withdrawal was not recorded.
12. It was assumed that no combined programmes of study involved subjects in ASC 1.

13. If the student subsequently switched to, say, a BA in Social Science (probably self-funding at least one bridging year) then the cost to the public purse of withdrawal/switching would be the difference between the total cost of funding the student through both the initial stages of the MEng and the final stages of the BA, and what it 'ought' to have cost to 'produce', straightforwardly, a graduate in Social Science.

14. There is a possibility that this figure might be on the high side, since those who 'felt good' about having returned to higher education might have been disproportionately likely to respond to the surveys (particularly the mail questionnaire). It will be recalled that a higher percentage of respondents to the mail questionnaire reported actually having returned to higher education, even though the percentage intending to complete a programme of higher education was almost identical for the two groups of respondents.

15. This assumption may be weakest in respect of ASC 1.

16. This is the best assumption that can be made since information relating to actual transfer was not available (and would require a substantial tracking study through the HESA record), and — obviously — there is no information relating to those students who were actively contemplating re-entry into higher education. The costs estimated here are at 1994–95 values.

17. In the experience of the six institutions in the north-west of England, this is not unreasonable as an estimate.

18. If higher education were in the business of manufacturing widgets, a different view might hold sway.

19. Some of the differences between ASCs can be attributed to entry qualification.

20. Of course, there will be failures amongst those who return to higher education — but these have not been estimated here.

21. The working assumption here is that, after means testing, about one-third of the student population would pay the full contribution to tuition fees (£1000 in 1998), one-third would pay half the contribution and one-third would pay nothing. No allowance has been made for any costs arising from default on student loans or deferral of repayment.

22. In February 1998, at a conference organized by the Society for Research into Higher Education, the initial findings of the pilot study were presented by John Thompson and Mark Corver of HEFCE.

23. At the time of completing this book HEFCE was consulting institutions with a view to verifying the accuracy of the data from the analysis prior to publishing a report.

Chapter 7

Non-completion as a Performance Indicator?

Orientation

This chapter opens by listing four questions which the user of performance indicators ought to address, and acknowledges that practical considerations have a bearing on what might be used as an indicator. Two studies of the use of (non-)completion data as performance indicators are then reviewed. The conclusions drawn from these studies are used to underpin propositions regarding how non-completion data might be used as performance indicators, and the propositions are subsequently subjected to empirical investigation. Some comments are made about the implications for institutional record systems of the proposed methods of calculating non-completion rates, and the chapter ends by recommending indicators which are likely to be particularly useful within the higher education sector.

Performance indicators

Given that non-completion constitutes a cost on the public purse (though probably it will be seen to be a smaller cost after 1998 when the change from the student maintenance award to a loan has bedded down), non-completion has an obvious attraction as a potential performance indicator. It could be brought into the mechanism for funding institutions, with institutions exhibiting high non-completion rates being penalized for apparently poor performance. However, before reaching a conclusion on the utility of non-completion as a performance indicator, consideration has to be given to four questions (Yorke, 1998a):

- Who wants to know what?
- For what purposes is the information to be used?
- How valid and reliable are the indicators that are being used or are being proposed for use?
- Do the indicators have any side effects?

Where institutions are publicly funded, the government will aim to ensure that the costs of non-completion are as low as can reasonably be achieved, and it will wish to steer institutions towards this end, perhaps through the funding mechanism. Institutions need to know what the non-completion rates are, at both gross institutional and sub-institutional levels, for a variety of purposes including budgeting and the improvement of quality in a number of different respects. Prospective students might take notice of completion or non-completion rates if they appear in guides to choosing universities.

As was noted in Chapter 1, data on non-completion have been notable for their lack of robustness: definitions (both explicit and implicit) have varied, and the ways in which institutions have collected and presented data have not been standardized. Even under the HESA requirements for reporting data there appears to have been scope for variability in reporting — and so conclusions from the HESA database have to be drawn with considerable caution. The pictures one can currently discern are probably more akin to an impressionist painting than a crisp photograph.

Some sharpening of the image may be possible as data collection and compilation is refined, but extreme precision may prove to be subject to the law of diminishing returns. As Ewell and Jones (1994, p. 16) put it:

> Many promising indicator systems fail simply because they are too expensive, too complex, too time-consuming, or too politically costly to implement. Often the simplest is the best, even if it initially seems less technically attractive.

Ewell and Jones are using the language of compromise here. Given the complexity of dealing with non-completion in practical terms, this language will reappear as the implications of using non-completion as a performance indicator are discussed further.

What about side effects? An indicator that is to be used across the higher education system should ideally be neutral with respect to institutions, i.e. it ought not advantage one type of institution over another. In practice, the ideal is very difficult to achieve since institutional missions vary in a system that claims diversity as a virtue. Research on the 'league tables' of universities produced by *The Times* shows that these have been dominated by research, resourcing (and probably reputation), and that communitarian values have been backgrounded (see Yorke, 1997a, 1998b). Non-completion is problematic as an indicator because differences in institutional mission are reflected in the kinds of student that are attracted. An institution seeking to attract 'second chance' students risks a higher non-completion rate if such students find that, after all, they are — for whatever reason — unable to cope with the expectations of curricula in higher education. With the present Labour government committed to widening access, it would not wish to see institutions 'playing safe' by limiting entry to those who could, *a priori*, be expected to complete their programmes successfully. Put another way, the use of non-completion as a performance indicator (in order to exert some restraint on costs) might work to the disadvantage of other policy objectives, such as the widening of access to higher education.

For the moment it is necessary to refrain from coming to firm conclusions regarding the utility of non-completion as a performance indicator as earlier work on the issue and empirical investigations throw additional light on the subject.

Previous research on indicators of (non-)completion

The Linke Report in Australia (Linke, 1991) investigated the feasibility of a number of performance indicators, amongst them being two that are of relevance here — the Student Progress Rate and the Program Completion Rate (PCR).[1] The version of the former that was adopted in the Australian system, under the title Study Progress Unit (SPU), is calculated simply as the ratio of the sum of the units passed to the sum of the units in which the student was assessed. This ratio could be calculated equally easily on the basis of the individual student and of groups of students. Although Linke and his colleagues unearthed some practical problems with this indicator (such as determining the completion status of some students) they concluded that:

> Despite the limitations in scope this analysis clearly illustrates the capacity of the indicator to reveal systematic differences in student progress rate between different academic organisational units [AOUs] . . . and within any particular AOU between different levels of study.
>
> (Linke, 1991, vol. 1, p. 67)

The Student Progress Unit has been used in an analysis of the relationship between students' backgrounds and their first-year performances in the Australian higher education system (Dobson et al., 1996).

Linke and his colleagues had greater difficulty with the PCR. They tried to cumulate the retention rates for successive years by multiplying the rates together and by multiplying the first-year retention rate by various exponents of the average annual retention rate for subsequent years. Despite the difficulties that became apparent with this indicator (which derived, *inter alia*, from the wide variation in initial retention rate, student transfer, the cumulation of errors especially in respect of longer programmes, and the particular problems posed by part-time students) they felt able to recommend that the PCR be defined for full-time students as follows:

$$\text{Estimated PCR} = \text{IRR} \, (\text{ACR})^{n-2}$$

where IRR is the initial retention rate, ACR is the average annual continuation rate and n is the length of the programme in years.[2]

The exponent $n - 2$ was chosen on technical grounds relating to the dates at which student enrolment is logged in Australia. The original choice of $n - 1$ would have been consistent with the full span of the course (IRR covering the first year), but the census date of 31 March meant that virtually all final year students enrolled on that date would graduate (i.e. the continuation rate for the final year would be near to unity), and hence the use of $n - 1$ in the formula would underestimate PCR. It was acknowledged, however, that in some instances the final year success rate could be rather less than unity, in which case the formula for PCR would give rise to an overestimate. Other formulae were recommended for programmes of one and two years duration.[3]

In the UK the Joint Performance Indicators Working Group (JPIWG) recommended a number of macro-level indicators (JPIWG, 1994a, pp. 68–70),[4] amongst them the following.

- *Completion with qualifications*, defined as:

$$\frac{\text{Number of students leaving with qualifications}}{\text{Number of students leaving}}$$

This ratio can be calculated with respect to gender and to different age groups.

- *Completion with good standing* (i.e. the proportion of those deemed fit to progress to the succeeding year), defined as:

$$\frac{\text{Number of students completing a year in good standing}}{\text{Number of students enrolled}}$$

Likewise, this ratio can be calculated with respect to gender and to different age groups.

The JPIWG proposed the calculation of the two progression indicators on the basis of the 'census method'. Instead of using longitudinal data from a single cohort (which would take a long time to collect), data from a single academic year are used to construct an estimate of the longitudinal progression rate. In the explanatory and statistical material prepared by the Group to accompany its Consultative Report, there are examples which show how the census method is intended to work (see JPIWG, 1994b).

Non-completion is calculated as the sum of the 'unable to progress' rates (it would have been better to have written 'did not progress or complete', which would have clearly subsumed academic failure and withdrawal) for the years of the programme. For the first year, the ratio of 'non-progressors' to original cohort size is straightforward. For the second year, the true ratio of year 2 'non-progressors' to original year 2 numbers is multiplied by the proportion of the contemporaneous year 1 students who progress, and the multiplicative formula is extended for other contemporaneous years. Thus for a three-year programme the census non-completion rate is as follows:[5]

$$\frac{\text{NotP1}}{N(\text{yr1})} + \left[\frac{\text{P1}}{N(\text{yr1})} \times \frac{\text{NotP2}}{N(\text{yr2})} \right] + \left[\frac{\text{P1}}{N(\text{yr1})} \times \frac{\text{P2}}{N(\text{yr2})} \times \frac{\text{NotP3}}{N(\text{yr3})} \right]$$

where   'NotPX' terms refer to the numbers of students who did not progress from year X (and, in the case of NotP3, did not complete their programme successfully); 'P' terms refer to the numbers of students who did progress; and the 'N(yr)' terms refer to the numbers of students commencing each of the years of study.

It seems to have escaped the originator(s) of this formula that it can be simplified to

$$1 - (\text{Progression rate for Year } 1 \times \text{Progression rate for Year } 2 \times \ldots \times \text{Completion rate for Year } n)$$

where n is the number of years scheduled for the programme.

Table 7.1   Hypothetical data relating to three years of a programme in a particular academic year

Year of the programme	Number enrolled	Number successful	Number unsuccessful
1	100	90	10
2	94	86	8
3	88	83	5

Suppose that, for a three-year programme in a particular academic year, the success rates of students are as shown in Table 7.1. The simplified formula immediately above gives a non-completion rate of:

$$1 - (0.900 \times 0.915 \times 0.943)$$

or 0.223 (using three significant figures). Readers with an enthusiasm for mathematics are invited to confirm that the more complicated method of calculation gives the same result.

The underlying principle of the census approach has some similarity to that which underlies the Linke (1991) recommendations in that the use of cross-sectional data for estimation purposes is seen as getting over the difficulties associated with the longitudinal approach. In both the Linke and JPIWG formulae a compromise between accuracy and usability is being struck. However, the Linke formula suffers from a relatively rapid diminution with increasing number of years, and the resulting indexes seem to reflect reality rather poorly. On this count, the JPIWG formulation seems preferable.

What about the side effects? The main problem for institutions is the first-year non-progression rate, which is typically much larger than that of subsequent years. For the 1994–95 student body as a whole, the mean yearly non-completion rate recorded by HESA declined from 10.1 per cent in the first year to 3.8 and 1.6 per cent in the two succeeding years, though the way in which these data were collected makes it likely that they underestimate the true figures by roughly a factor of two. The first of these HESA figures (particularly) is likely to submerge considerable inter-institutional variation (see Johnes and Taylor, 1990a), part of which will reflect institutional policies regarding entry. The use of the JPIWG formula (and, *a fortiori*, the Linke formula) for purposes which might impact on institutional behaviour is therefore problematic: as noted earlier, an institution with a strong access policy might be discouraged from pursuing it as vigorously as it might otherwise do.

Three approaches to the calculation of non-completion

There seem to be three main units of analysis in considering non-completion, each of which relates to a 'natural' phase of a student's experience in higher education — the programme as a whole, the year (or, perhaps more usefully for part-time students, the *level*) of study and the study unit itself. For some programmes, such as many taught Master's programmes, the first two coincide. The difficulty is that the three units of analysis do not quite fit together, since students may be successful in study units or year/level but choose to discontinue during the period between components of their experience. This dislocation is captured schematically in Figure 7.1.

Figure 7.1 *A schematic representation of the relationship between progression and departure, ignoring the complications that stem from entry into the programme some time after it has started. The squares symbolize study units or modules*

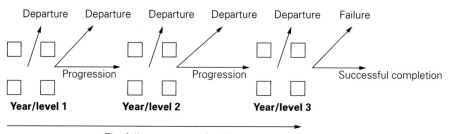

From Figure 7.1 it is apparent that the completion rate for the full programme is highly likely to be lower than the 'per year' progression rate, and that a similar relationship holds between the rate of progression 'per year' and that of the study unit. Inter-year departure is a problem as student non-returners may not be captured in data submitted to HESA.

Before considering whether there exists a 'best buy' for the unit of analysis of non-completion it is necessary to examine each in a little more detail.

The full programme non-completion rate

The advantage of this measure is that it does produce answers to questions such as 'What proportion of entering medical students fails to qualify?' A major disadvantage of using the full programme as the unit of analysis is that the programme may, because of unitization, not be easily identifiable. If the programme is contained within the boundaries of an ASC, then it is possible to consider the ASC as the unit of analysis, though precision (which, depending on the nature of the subjects taken, may or may not be important) will inevitably be reduced. Another major disadvantage is the length of time it takes to collect the data, even if students stick to the expected programme duration. This period is extended if, as is the case for measurement purposes in the US, 50 per cent more than the expected time is allowed for students to complete.[6] If the system is sufficiently flexible to allow students to build up credits over a number of years, possibly by mixing periods of full-time study with part-time study and allowing intercalations, the time to completion becomes very large. It is typically larger for part-time students than full-time students.[7] It will be recalled from Chapter 2 that, in the United States (where flexibility in attendance is high), the *completion* rate for bachelor's degrees in a national sample of relevant institutions crept up from 39.9 per cent at four years after enrolment to 45.7 per cent after nine years (Astin et al., 1996).

A further disadvantage with the full programme non-completion rate is that it does not allow any estimate to be made of the distinction between various causes of non-completion (for example, between failure and withdrawal despite passing all the relevant assessments).

From the point of view of policy making, the full programme non-completion rate may become of decreasing usefulness in a UK system whose flexibility regarding participation is edging towards that of the US and Australia.

The year/level non-completion rate

For full-time students at least, the time it takes for the relevant information to become available is tightly under control. This was the underpinning attraction of the census approach proposed by the JPIWG. Part-time students can be expected to take more than a year to cover the ground that their full-time peers cover in a year, and hence the period of time to complete a study level is more likely to be useful. There are two difficulties, however. Part-time students will take different times to complete a level, and so the 'level non-completion' measure for these students suffers similar disadvantages — though typically on a lesser scale — to those that the full programme non-completion rate has in respect of full-time students. Moreover, part-time students (to a greater extent than their full-time peers) may study units from different levels at the same time.

Cumulation of the year *progression* rate for full-time students into the census method for non-completion (see the formula presented earlier on p. 84) does appear to have some practical value provided that the data for the year progression rate are commensurate. This caveat is necessary since some may calculate the rate on the basis of the end-of-year examinations whereas others may base it on the position after any resit examinations have been taken. Further, inter-year withdrawal of successful students may or may not be taken into account. Assuming commensurate data, then, the census method offers the possibility of benchmarking comparisons regarding (non-)completion, which could be useful to institutions as they attempt to identify problems and to make improvements. To maximize the accuracy of the census-based index as an estimate of non-completion, it would be necessary to build in any inter-year withdrawal by students who had ended the year 'in good standing', though, to date, this has proved difficult for some institutions.

The study unit non-completion rate

The measure here is simple: students succeed or not on the unit. Causes of non-completion, other than academic failure, will in the main lie outside the scope of the measure.[8] Modern information systems have no difficulty in handling the amount of data that a unitized programme throws up and are capable of producing analyses by study unit, institutional sub-unit and so on. It is easy to compare (non-)completion rates at the level at which any desired remedial action can be set in motion. For example, a mathematics unit which has a student success rate of, say, only 50 per cent ought to trigger some form of investigation into why the rate was so low. It could raise questions such as whether the specified prerequisites were inappropriate or whether the teaching approach was not well tailored to the abilities of the students.

An investigation of the three approaches to calculating non-completion

The empirical study

In order to explore further the three indexes of non-completion, a small-scale study was made of results from one three-year full-time programme running in a post-1992 university. The cohort entering in the autumn of 1992 was selected and cross-sectional data was also collected for the academic year 1994–95. This programme was part of the university's credit scheme which required at that time 90 credits for the award of an honours degree and 75 credits for an unclassified degree. Full-time students normally took modules to the total of 30 credits each year.

The longitudinal data for the cohort entering in 1992 were analysed with reference to three levels of measurement — the full programme completion rate, the progression rates for each year[9] and the completion rate for the unit of study. The last of these presented a particular problem since there are two ways of approaching it: one can look at the *module* or *unit* completion rate in a manner similar to that adopted in Australia (the study progress unit, SPU), or in terms of the ratio of credits gained to credits taken. Since the module sizes vary in the credit scheme, the number of modules taken has little significance — the number of credits is the key measure, even though the number of credits per module varies. The decision was made that the number of credits was the more appropriate measure. This meant that some modules were 'weighing more heavily' in the calculation of the completion rate, but there was no way of avoiding a compromise of this sort whichever approach had been adopted. Where a student had resat an assessment successfully, this result was taken as satisfying the criterion of credit(s) gained.[10]

Inspection of the data revealed some ambiguous situations which had presumably been resolved by the relevant examination board. For example, a few students seemed to have been allowed to progress despite not having attained the number of credits expected for progression, and two ended up with a total of only 89 credits, even though they had attained 30 credits in their final year. In Table 7.2 the ambiguous performances are assigned to a separate category, and the two students with 89 credits have been assigned to the unclassified degree category, even though it is likely that the final examination board will have recommended the award of a degree with honours. In practice, however, these difficulties make no difference to the nature of the analysis.

The overall completion data in Table 7.3 do not tally exactly with Table 7.2 because of the ambiguities that were discerned — for example, a student who gained 30 credits in the final year may have gained fewer than 60 in the preceding two years combined, and a student may have been able to rectify in the second year a deficiency in the number of credits from the first year. Nevertheless, there is a fairly close correspondence between the data in Tables 7.2 and 7.3.

The apparent non-completion rate for the cohort of 77 students whose details are given in Table 7.2 is therefore 0.18. This figure does not take into account the eight students who appear to have joined the cohort after the first year as the cross-sectional sample of third-year students in 1994–95 totalled 78 (see Table 7.4 below). Had these students been included, having been accorded notional successful completion for prior studies elsewhere, the apparent non-completion rate would have been 14 out of (77 + 8), or 0.16. It should be noted that, in contradistinction to the transferring of students *into* an institution, transfers out would affect the overall completion rate adversely. In a higher education system which is not unfavourably disposed towards transfer, this — as was noted earlier — is a weakness of the index.

The 1994–95 cross-sectional data are summarized in Table 7.4. Using from earlier the formula

$$1 - (\text{Progression rate for Year 1} \times \text{Progression rate for Year 2} \times \text{Completion rate for Year 3})$$

the data in Table 7.4 give a census non-completion rate of 0.30.

Leaving Early

Table 7.2 'Per year' completion rates for a cohort of students in the credit scheme (the proportions in the table relate to the particular year)

Year	No. of students	30 credits passed		Ambiguous achievement		Failure to complete year	
		N	Proportion	N	Proportion	N	Proportion
1	77	70	0.91	2	0.03	5	0.06
2	72	63	0.88	7	0.10	2	0.03
3	70	57	0.81	5	0.07	8	0.11

Table 7.3 Outcomes for the 1992 student cohort: the awards are notional in that they are based on the module records rather than on what the final examination board might have decided

N of students	Awarded honours degree		Awarded unclassified degree		No degree awarded	
	N	Proportion	N	Proportion	N	Proportion
77	55	0.71	8	0.10	14	0.18

Table 7.4 'Per year' completion rates for the cross-sectional students in 1994–95: in year 3, 15–29 credits gained would normally be expected to lead to the award of an unclassified degree

Year (level) of study	Number of students	Number gaining 30 credits	Number gaining fewer than 30 credits		Year completion rate
			Number gaining 15–29 credits	Number gaining fewer than 15 credits	
1	79	72	7		0.91
2	74	63	11		0.85
3	78	61	10	7	0.91*

* Implies that a successful outcome is a degree, classified or otherwise.

The credit completion rates for both samples of students are shown in Table 7.5.

Table 7.5   *Credit completion rates for the 1992 longitudinal and 1994–95 cross-sectional samples (see the text for a comment on the accuracy of the year/level 3 data)*

Sample of students	Year (level) 1	Year (level) 2	Year (level) 3
1992 cohort	0.93	0.89	0.84
1994–95 cross-section	0.92	0.96	0.85

Implications for student record systems

This exploration showed that the institutional student record system had no difficulty in principle regarding the furnishing of relevant data for the calculation of the three indexes. However, if it were to be used for these purposes, some changes to operating procedures would need to be implemented.[11]

As it is currently operated, the record system only keeps on permanent file the record of students' assessments, the record of the modules/credits for which the student was registered being expunged once the diet of assessments (including resits, where appropriate) has been completed and the outcomes logged. It was therefore impossible to obtain a reliable figure for the modules/credits for which students had been registered and, for the purposes of this investigation, an estimate had to be made of the number of credits taken by the student (this would normally be 30, but some students had exceeded this number — possibly as an insurance policy against failing one or more modules[12]). The error involved in the first and second years is probably quite small, but is likely to be quite large in the third year, where some students may have chosen to aim for an unclassified degree and hence to have attempted 15(+) credits rather than the 30 that would be needed for an honours degree. Lacking any record of the original credit registrations, the assumption was made that any student completing years 1 and 2 with a total of 60 credits would aim for honours. It is unlikely that this assumption is tenable in every case since there is a strong suspicion that some students may have registered only for the 15 credits necessary for the degree (ten in the longitudinal study appear not to have gone forward for assessment in respect of the major project, worth nine credits). Hence the completion rates for the third year are very likely to underestimate the true completion rate.

Second, the record system would need to be more explicit about ambiguous cases such as those that this investigation threw up — for example, by flagging the reasons for the apparent progression of students who have not gained the number of credits (including compensation) normally required to proceed. For example, one student who apparently gained insufficient credit at level 1 in order to proceed to year 2 may have transferred in from another institution with a measure of credit for prior learning, but the record is not

explicit on this point. With attention to matters such as this, the yearly completion rate would be more sharply defined as a result.

Third, and of probably lesser importance, the student assessment record
may need to be refined. At present, it indicates that student resit performances
might have been considered at the relevant module examination board, even
though the student has not presented him- or herself for assessment. The system logs the fact that the student was eligible for reassessment without necessarily any expectation that he or she would actually appear on the relevant date.

A best buy?

Is there a 'best buy' from the three approaches to the calculation of non-
completion rate? There are advantages and disadvantages in respect of each. A
key criterion for the choice of index is the purpose(s) to which it is to be put.

The full programme non-completion rate, in the case of students who
have taken full-time or sandwich programmes (and whose studies may have
exceeded the expected length by a relatively limited amount) provides the
truest index. The 50 per cent extension permitted for the purposes of reporting
completions in the United States seems excessive when one considers that
some programmes in the United Kingdom run for six years. A criterion of
greater utility might be non-completion in $n + 1$ years, where n is the expected
length of the programme. This indicator, converted into a completion index,
provides information about the success rate of particular cohorts of students
(and hence of the higher education system in 'delivering' qualified people into
society) and, with due caution, allows questions of comparability to be raised.[13]
A weakness is the indicator's inability to deal adequately with the transfer of
successful students to other institutions, although transfers into institutions can
be accommodated.[14] For part-time students, the greater expected length of
their programmes reduces the utility of the full-programme non-completion rate.

A strong candidate is the study unit non-completion rate. This measure,
which is equally applicable to full-time and part-time students, deals with the
successes and failures of students in a way that is relatively uncluttered by non-
academic causes of non-completion such as financial difficulty or unhappiness
with the location of the institution. It also provides institutions with information
that can be used towards the improvement of their performance.

The year/level non-completion rate on its own seems to be the least
useful of the three in that it addresses key questions less well than the other
measures without offering any compensating advantages. Cumulating progression rates according to the census method, however, can provide, in respect
of full-time and sandwich students, an estimate of the true longitudinal
non-completion rate, and can accommodate the late entry of students on to
the programme more easily than the full programme non-completion rate. The
relatively quick production of the estimate of the longitudinal rate may well be
of greater advantage to policy makers than the greater accuracy of the true

rate, which can only be computed some time after the end of the programme in question.

All three suffer from one potential disadvantage. If the funding of institutions were to be connected to any of these indicators, there would be some risk to the maintenance of standards.[15] This could well be at its strongest for the study unit non-completion rate since, particularly at the lower levels, it would be difficult to build in adequate external checking because the external examiner system is widely acknowledged to be under strain (see, for example, Silver et al., 1995).[16] If these indicators are considered in their positive form (i.e. in relation to *completion* rather than non-completion), they are merely 'threshold' measures which do not take into account the standards that have been reached by students.

Conclusions

The preceding analysis suggests that two methods of calculating non-completion rate are likely to have some practical applicability within the sector.

The first is the proportion of full-time and sandwich students who do not complete the programme for which they were enrolled. This addresses the question of the relationship between what the state and other funders invest in, and the success of that investment. Students who switch to other programmes would, for the purposes of this definition, be treated as having withdrawn, but transferees in could be accommodated by invoking the philosophy of the accreditation of prior learning (APL).

The simple conversion of the definition into an index is problematic. However, an estimate of the full programme non-completion rate (and hence of the extent to which the original qualification aim has not been achieved) can be obtained by using the yearly progression/completion rates according to the JPIWG's (1994b) census method, provided that this is undertaken to a standard format — for example, by insisting on a common approach to inter-year withdrawal. For some students, the nature of the programme is unambiguous (e.g. Medicine, Dentistry), whereas for others a looser categorization — perhaps as loose as the ASC — may be all that can be used.[17] Transfers in and out of the programme do not cause difficulty since the index is based on 'per year' success rates. The virtue of the index is the speed with which the index can be computed, which weighs strongly when set against the inaccuracies that are likely to inhere in it. Useful, but a little rough, information now is of more practical value than near-perfect information that takes a long time to arrive — another way of making Ewell and Jones's (1994) point noted above. However, the use of the raw index without reference to contextual variables could — as Johnes and Taylor (1990a) make clear — do injustices to institutions.

The second definition is the 'micro-version': the proportion of study units in which a group of students does not pass the assessment. This definition is convertible easily into an index and is applicable to all modes of study. It has the further advantage of probably eliminating from consideration most of the non-academic reasons for withdrawal and thus focuses on the success or otherwise of the student in terms of the programme's demands. This index is likely to be a truer index of the ineffectiveness of the student/institution partnership but leaves open the issue of the apportionment of blame for failure. The potential for benchmarking and contribution to improvement within the institution is relatively high as it tackles the issue of non-success at the level at which any necessary remedial action is potentially most easily identified.

Where the programme is unitized but not based on a credit framework, the study unit is the unit of analysis. Where a credit system is in operation and the number of credits per unit varies, the number of credits is probably to be preferred as the dominant measure as far as student performance is concerned, and in this case the index should be computed with reference to the proportion of credits gained rather than the proportion of modules or units, even though this has some technical limitations.

The key to applying both of these methods satisfactorily lies in institutional student record systems which may need adaptation if reliable data are to be produced.

Finally, and importantly, the use of the output-related indexes in respect of funding could give rise to adverse effects on academic standards. The important issue is the extent to which institutions deal with the indexes of performance that they collect. An improvement-oriented quality assurance system in which institutions are asked how they are using to good purpose the information they collect would, in contrast, be likely to have little, if any, adverse effect on standards.[18]

Notes

1. See Linke (1991), vol. 1, pp. 66–78 and Appendix 8.
2. A caveat was entered that the number of students should be at least 20 in each of enrolment, continuation and completion (Linke, 1991, vol. 1, p. 76).
3. See Linke (1991), vol. 1, p. 77.
4. See also CVCP (1995) (which subsumes the JPIWG Consultative report), p. 51. For qualifying comments to the indicators, see the notes in the original text.
5. This is presented differently from — and perhaps more clearly than — the example in JPIWG (1994b).
6. In her study Johnes (1990) used as an index completion in six years of commencement, but this does not take into account that the normal length of some programmes varies with the subject studied. Such an index is unsuitable for part-time students.
7. In the UK Open University, which has a part-time student body, the problem of students not reaching graduation (55 per cent of finally-registered students) was acknowledged to be an issue that the university has to address (Rickwood et al., 1995).

8. Personal mitigating circumstances or some form of institutional maladministration could come into consideration here in respect of unsuccessful performance.

9. In the case of the third year, this was the third-year *completion* rate.

10. This was fair to the student and anyway necessary as the database overwrote failed credits with subsequent success.

11. If the completion rates were computed immediately after the assessment process was completed, then the retention of the registration data would not be a problem unless the auditing of institutional claims about performance (necessarily retrospective) were for any reason to be implemented.

12. In the early days of the credit scheme this was not uncommon. However, the economic implications of this practice led to its discouragement by the institution.

13. That caution is needed is shown by the work of Chapman (1994) and HEQC (1996a) where persistent differences in degree class were shown to exist between institutions, though the causes of these differences are more difficult to determine.

14. The admission of students to later stages of the programme can be resolved by giving them a notional successful completion for the year(s) they have missed. A philosophical justification analogous to that for the accreditation of prior learning could be applied.

15. See Cave et al. (1997, pp. 137–42) for a discussion which includes the problematic nature of the progression rate as a performance indicator.

16. External examiners tend to have relatively little to do with first-year (or level 1) performances.

17. Mixed programmes might have to be treated in terms of 'blanket' categories such as mixed Humanities and Social Science, mixed Science-based studies, and mixed Humanities/Social Science and Science-based studies.

18. See, on this point, Yorke (1997b).

Chapter 8

What Can be Done about Non-completion?

Orientation

The chapter begins with a number of caveats relating to the findings of the surveys. The findings are then discussed with reference to various aspects of the research surveys, which are grouped with reference to 'the student experience', background characteristics of students, and effectiveness and efficiency. The subdivisions in this chapter are not particularly 'tidy' since the components overlap each other at a number of points. During the discussion markers are laid down regarding the sources of possible action designed to reduce non-completion where this is feasible, and these markers are brought together in a section which concentrates on strategies aiming at the improvement of retention. In an inversion of the sequence of Chapter 2, the empirical then gives way to the theoretical, with Tinto's theorizing being revisited in the light of the empirical evidence that has been presented. A short coda revisits the empirical deficit and indicates ways forward for research.

Three caveats

Any research which relies on self-reporting has to bear in mind the potential for lack of objectivity, psychological self-defence and so on.[1] Realities are not always what they are purported to be. The issue of response bias is perhaps less of a problem for the research reported here than for the majority of other studies as a telephone survey was conducted in respect of those who did not return the first mail questionnaire. As noted earlier, although the *patterns* of response from the two groups were broadly similar, the responses to the telephone survey were, however, significantly different from those of the preceding mail survey in the *strength* of a number of influences. The possibility of response bias has clearly not been eliminated (those who chose not to respond to both surveys could still be different), but the double methodology used in respect of the 1994–95 withdrawers has probably reduced it. It will be recalled that the mail survey of the 1995–96 withdrawers was not followed by a telephone survey.

The second caveat is that, in concentrating on those who did not complete programmes for which they were enrolled, the research dealt with a particular group of students rather than a representative sample of the student body. To base policy solely on the outcomes of a study of withdrawers and not to include a consideration of those students who did complete their studies would be rather akin to a national government framing legislation on the basis of the opinions of a few self-selected focus groups.

The third caveat relates to scale and generalizability. HESA data for 1994–95 indicate that there was a lower recorded rate of withdrawal (4.7 per cent) of full-time and sandwich students from the six institutions in this project than for English institutions as a whole (5.4 per cent).[2] The latter figure was heavily influenced by the London region, whose withdrawal rate is recorded as 7.1 per cent. There are a number of reasons for variation in the influences on withdrawal, some of which may be hidden in regional-level statistics. Small, specialist colleges and community-oriented universities, for example, have characteristics that might well lead to different weightings being given to the various influences on withdrawal that were found in this study of six strongly urban institutions in the north-west of England.

Nevertheless, the findings from the present study probably offer a reasonable basis for generalization at the 'macro' level and for useful comparisons for institutions both similar to, and different from, those involved in this research.

The discussion below draws on the findings from the research and works its way — obliquely to begin with — towards the addressing of non-completion at three levels, those of the student, the institution and the sector.[3]

Features of the student experience

The choice of study programme

Much that has been written about students' reasons for withdrawal is supported by this study.[4] The findings from this study suggest that some full-time and sandwich students have an insufficiently well-developed sense of the direction they want to take to justify an immediate transition from school to higher education. They may well benefit from bucking a middle class expectation of education as an unbroken continuum from nursery or primary school to higher education. Both parents and those in the schools sector who are responsible for advising on careers may do their charges a greater service by explaining the virtues of not rushing into higher education without a sense of commitment, for this research has turned up plenty of evidence that showed that, for withdrawers, the choice process was deficient.[5] Those who were able to secure paid employment would have the additional possibility of building up a reserve of finance to help them through their period in higher education, which might reduce their chances of withdrawing on financial grounds.

Not all should be left to advisers in respect of careers: the intending student him- or herself has a responsibility to find out whether the programme he or she envisages following is as imagined. What appears on paper in prospectuses and guides to universities (or is passed on relatively informally) is only a fraction of the information that will be needed for a soundly grounded choice — and this research has produced evidence to call into doubt the quality of some of the information that students have received.[6] Students need to satisfy themselves regarding the nature and location of the programme, and the institution has a responsibility to make sure that the information that is provided is accurate and not economical with the truth. For both parties to the 'deal', it is no good a student accepting a place on a Mathematics degree only to find that its heavily theoretical orientation does not accord with his or her bent for solving practical problems, or for a student to find out too late that the programme is being run on a relatively remote site.

The data presented in this book are consistent with what has been established about those who enter higher education some time after the age of 18 (whether on a full-time or a part-time basis) — that they generally have a better idea of what they want to do and where they want to do it.

Of the full-time and sandwich students who responded to the surveys, 44 per cent of those in the pre-1992 universities (compared with 38 per cent in post-1992 universities and 34 per cent in the colleges) indicated that they had made the wrong choice of field of study. These figures were almost exactly mirrored in the proportions who indicated a lack of commitment to their programmes (43 per cent, 36 per cent and 35 per cent, respectively).[7] There is also a link of institutional type to age and social class, with young, middle class students contributing a greater proportion of withdrawals from the pre-1992 universities. There is a question for all institutions, but particularly for the pre-1992 universities as their profiles of entrants are the most heavily weighted with younger students, about the extent to which intending students are apprised about the realities of the study programmes on which they are seeking to embark: to what extent would better information from the institutions help to reduce the mismatch between student and study programme? Could information of this sort overcome the concern expressed by Roberts and Allen (1996) about prospective students' lack of knowledge of the higher education system which they are seeking to join? There may be potential for institutions to be more active in seeking to achieve an optimal match between student and programme — a matter that seems to be of greatest importance for those entering higher education direct from school.[8]

The evidence of withdrawers suggests that the choosing of programmes of study (or, for 'Clearing' students, institutions) could be improved, and that the improvement might be greatest for the pre-1992 universities simply because their intakes tend to be younger and perhaps have a relatively unformed basis for their choice. There seem to be three ways in which the problem might be addressed.

1. Better advice could be made available to pupils who are preparing to enter higher education. The guess might be hazarded with some confidence that many students who do well at school continue, 'naturally' (and in some cases under parental pressure), into higher education without undertaking a searching analysis of what they want to do and why they want to do it. This 'natural progression' (which certainly existed for some of the students in the surveys reported in this book) may have contributed to the manifested student dissatisfaction with the choice of programme.

2. There may be scope for institutions to make more clear to intending students what it is that they are offering. Prospectuses have taken on some of the characteristics of travel brochures and may set up presumptions and expectations that visits are unable to dispel.[9] Anecdotal evidence suggests that institutions (or, probably more accurately, academic units) vary quite considerably in the extent to which they communicate to intending students what the nature of the proposed programme is. Being explicit about 'the deal' between institution and student is likely to minimize dissatisfaction, and is a component of quality that some institutions have sought to recognize in their production of student charters.

3. The rapidity with which students have to cope with the Clearing process is unlikely to be conducive to measured choice of study programme or institution, particularly when the intending student's preferred choice is not available. It was noted in Chapter 4 that students entering through Clearing tended to be more dissatisfied with aspects of institutional provision, but that this dissatisfaction did not extend to programmes of study. This rather surprising finding regarding programmes has at least two possible causes. First, it may be the case that some respondents have been hazy about what Clearing actually was and the data are simply contaminated by this. Second, the marked differences with regard to three institutional variables (the institution itself, computing and specialist equipment) hint that the students were clear about the subject(s) they wanted to study[10] but rather less so about the institution in which they wanted to study — after all, many at that time are hastily revising their expectations regarding entry to higher education in the light of A-level performances that do not satisfy the requirements of conditional offers. The balance between the two possible causes may lie towards the second, but this is a matter which needs further study.

    If there is something in the proposition that the institution (if not the programme) is not clearly perceived by students during the Clearing process, then this adds a little weight to the calls that have been made for the application and admissions process to be reformed in order to allow a greater time to elapse between the publishing of the A-level results and the admission of students to institutions.

The quality of the learning experience

An issue of concern to many withdrawers (full-time and sandwich, and part-time male, students) appears to be the quality of their learning experiences in higher education. It is quite easy to dismiss claims of unsatisfactory teaching on the grounds of *post hoc* rationalization, but the work of Seymour and Hewitt (1997) in the fields of Science, Mathematics and Engineering should give pause for thought as they established, from a sample which contained both persisters and withdrawers, that the teaching of these subjects in the United States often exhibited characteristics which were inimical to good learning. It seems distinctly possible that their findings can be translated, *mutatis mutandis*, into other subject areas and into the context of the United Kingdom. It is appropriate to recall, yet again, that the act of teaching is not necessarily followed by good learning.

Differences between ASCs

When the distribution of withdrawals across subject areas (here represented rather grossly by HEFCE Academic Subject Categories) is examined, some marked differences emerge (Table 8.1). In ASC 10 (Art, Design and the Performing Arts) withdrawing students were more likely than the general body of respondents to indicate that the reason for withdrawal was related to the learning experience. To a lesser extent, but still more than the average, the same tended to be true of students from ASC 1 (Clinical and Pre-clinical subjects),[11] ASC 4 (Engineering and Technology) and ASC 5 (Built Environment), and of those students who had been following mixed programmes. In contrast stood ASC 11 (Education) and ASC 8 (Social Science) and, to a lesser extent, ASC 2 (Subjects and Professions Allied to Medicine) and ASC 9 (Humanities). Perhaps not unexpectedly, lack of academic progress was cited as an influence on withdrawal more frequently in ASCs 1, 4, 5 and 10, and less frequently in ASCs 8 (Social Science) and 11 (Education). Students in ASC 10 were (not surprisingly, given the conditions of entry to this ASC) less likely to feel that they had made the wrong choice of field of study and less likely to have felt the need for a break from education. Students taking mixed science-based programmes were more likely to have felt that they had made the wrong choice of programme and to have found their programmes not to have been what they had expected.

There is something of a pattern in these data, but there is a danger of an over-interpretation akin to that made by the early astronomers who perceived canals on Mars. Nevertheless, the data do tend to fit with what is known about the sector. There are hints here that programmes constructed from components from different ASCs tended not to be what these students expected, and that their learning experiences left something to be desired. Students in ASCs 8 and 11 generally cited fewer reasons than their peers for their withdrawal. Students from ASC 11, more than any other subject group, indicated that the

Table 8.1   Citation of influences on withdrawal by full-time and sandwich students, for items loading heavily on Factors 1, 2 and 4 (for each item, individual ASCs are compared against the overall mean)

Variable	Academic Subject Category													
	1	2	3	4	5	6	7	8	9	10	11	50	51	52
Quality of the teaching	–	++		+	+			–	–	++	–	+		
Inadequate staff support outside timetable	++			–						+	–	+		+
Organization of the programme	++								–	++	–	+		
Teaching did not suit me	+			+				–		++	–			
Lack of personal support from staff	++		++	++						+	–			+
Class size too large	–	+							–				+	–
Timetabling did not suit	–	+		++	–				–			+		++
Stress related to the programme	++			+									++	–
Difficulty of the programme	++		+	++		++								
Workload too heavy	++	+	+	++	++	++				–		–	+	
Lack of study skills		–		++		+				––		––		–
Lack of personal support from students	–	–			+	–					–	++		–
Insufficient academic progress	++	–		++	+					+	–		+	–
Chose wrong field of study	+		+							–				
Programme not relevant to career								––		–			+	+
Lack of commitment to programme	+	–								–	––	–		
Programme not as expected	+							–		+	–		+	+
Needed a break from education	–									–			++	++

Key: + and ++ respectively indicate between 20% and 40%, and at least 40%, *above* the item mean.
– and –– respectively indicate between 20% and 40%, and at least 40%, *below* the item mean.

needs of their dependants had been influential in their withdrawal, which would seem to be a function of their age at entry.[12]

The cases of ASCs 1, 4, 5 and 10 might be felt at first glance to be fairly similar. However, when one looks below the data collected for this project and reflects on the general teaching approaches in use, one can perhaps differentiate ASC 10 from the rest, in that students in Art and Design tend to be given much greater flexibility in fulfilling the expectations laid down for them than are their peers in the other ASCs, the structures of whose programmes are more tightly defined in terms of both hourage of class contact and 'subject delivery'. Students in these four ASCs tend more than others to cite lack of academic progress as an influence on withdrawal. It might be conjectured that in ASCs 1, 4 and 5 this relates to a failure to cope with the variety of demands made of them, whereas in ASC 10 it relates to relative uncertainty as to what the expectations actually are (if, for example, originality is important, then only after the event can it be seen whether the student has been successful since it is a contradiction to pre-specify creative activity).

If these findings are echoed in the general body of students (for that, evidence going beyond that presented here is needed) then institutions will be well-placed to take action to alleviate the more important problems.

Personal misfortune

Some students were obviously taken over by events against which they were powerless — illness and other personal misfortunes were noted by some. The precarious financial existence of a small number of students came to light particularly in the telephone survey, where an event that precipitated withdrawal (such as the departure of a partner and the need to care for children) was revealed as leading to consequences which made re-engagement in higher education difficult. For example, two women in this position were forced to rely on social security for income, owed money to various sources as a result of their time in higher education, and could not get any further support which would enable them to restart their studies and acquire the qualifications that they saw as allowing them to escape from the poverty trap. Solving problems such as this is probably beyond the power of the individual student — and apparently beyond the capacity of the benefits system as well. There lingers an unease that a government committed to encouraging people into work may not be in a position to register the occasional ripples of individuals' difficulties against the broader groundswell of policy, and hence to create the conditions under which the aspirations of such students can be realized.

Financial problems

Financial problems were identified by 37 per cent of the full-time and sandwich students as a moderate or considerable influence on their withdrawal, and by 23 per cent of the part-time students. Full-time and sandwich students have, in recent years, necessarily contributed more of the costs of their education due to constraint on the maintenance award and an increasing expectation on the part of institutions that they contribute towards the cost of consumables.[13] At the same time, their basic living expenses have risen: rents have increased, and those students who need childcare facilities find it very difficult to purchase these at prices that they can afford from their existing finances. As a consequence, students are increasingly taking out loans and running overdrafts at banks (NUS, 1995). A face-to-face survey of more than 2000 undergraduates conducted by NatWest at seven university sites suggested that a third felt that their finances were out of control (NatWest, 1998) and that a quarter had not matured in their attitude towards money since going to university.

The so-called 'Access Funds' provided to institutions and other institutional sources of financial support are able to deal with only a proportion of the hardship claims made upon them. Many full-time and sandwich students, therefore, are taking jobs in parallel with their higher education studies in order to make ends meet (or, perhaps more accurately in the majority of cases, to bring the financial ends closer together). Probably only a few will have gone as far as the final-year full-time student who is said (perhaps apocryphally) to have taken a full-time secretarial job in order to keep her finances in an acceptable state whilst relying on friends to pass on details of what had taken place on the course; in any case, the growth in unitization of curricula makes such manoeuvres more difficult.

There has been a failure by some full-time and sandwich students fully to appreciate what enrolment actually implied for their personal financial position and, for others, the freedom from being away from home led to excesses that the students came later to regret. The charity Shelter, following an opinion poll which showed that only 10 per cent of a sample of over 1000 young people had received information to help them prepare for leaving home and that about half of the sample believed that their school or college should help prepare them to fend for themselves (see Shelter, 1997), has distributed a pack of materials to secondary schools in the hope that this will be of assistance in mitigating the difficulties. Intending students in higher education may well benefit from these materials — if schools can find time in their crowded curricula to use them.

Induction, academic guidance and advice

Following Tinto's (1993) concerns regarding socialization, it is perhaps as important for some students that institutions provide an orientation period in which they are inducted into the ways and expectations of higher education (which can differ substantially from those of school or access course, or from their imaginings from outside the higher education system).

As the unitization of curricula spreads through higher education, so there is a need for greater guidance for students to navigate their way through the schemes.[14] Institutions can look at the nature of the student experience in the many fields of study that they offer in order to assess the extent to which the students are genuinely engaged in their programmes. It is quite possible that some changes will be found necessary in the chosen approach to teaching and learning, and that some way will need to be found to retain a component of personal contact between staff and students. Given the pressures on higher education (which finds a response — not always well-measured — in the enthusiasm of some for technological solutions), the rethink of teaching and learning may well need to lead to radical rather than incremental change.[15] It was noted earlier, in the discussion of withdrawal from different ASCs, that there seemed to be some quite marked differences between the characteristics of ASCs as seen from the point of view of withdrawers, and there would seem to be an opportunity here for institutions to determine, in the light of the growing knowledge about the ways in which students best learn,[16] whether the programmes being offered maximize the potential for student success. One question here is the extent to which students feel that they belong to an institutional group when their learning experiences are modular in character. This was an issue that exercised Her Majesty's Inspectors as modular schemes began to get under way in the then polytechnics in the late 1980s and early 1990s, and seems to be even more pertinent now.

Some students leave their institutions because they feel they lack support: pressures of numbers are militating against the personal tutor system that used to be a standard feature of the higher education experience. Others are taking over part of the personal tutor's role — for example, those concerned with academic guidance through modular schemes. Others, such as counsellors, are in a position to play a crucial supporting role, as Rickinson's (1997) study suggests.

The advising of students about their progress and possible futures has always been a feature of higher education in the United Kingdom. Anecdotal evidence from a number of institutions suggests that the incidence of students seeking advice has risen in recent years, not least as a result of the difficulties that students have with finance. An institutional concern to minimize withdrawal needs, however, to be tempered by a recognition that, for some students, withdrawal is the most appropriate course of action. It would be unprofessional for an institution, with an eye to the funding implications of withdrawal, to exert undue pressure on a student to persist.

Institutional support services have come under increasing pressure in recent years as financial stringency has bitten. There are hints from around the system that some institutional managers have not calculated as thoroughly as they might have done the benefit/cost ratio from having a high-grade student support service. As can be seen from Chapter 6, withdrawal is costly to an institution. It takes few full-time or sandwich students to be encouraged to persist (if that is the proper professional course of action) for the cost of a counsellor or welfare officer to be justified in hard financial terms.

Chapter 5 showed that relatively few withdrawers from part-time pro-grammes turned to institutional student support services for advice prior to leaving. The reason for this is not apparent from the data, but it can be hypo-thesized that, since most of such staff are probably present only during the daytime, their accessibility to part-time students is relatively low. One way of demonstrating an institutional commitment to the quality of the part-time stu-dent's experience is through the availability of support services at times when such students are on site.

Return to study after withdrawal

The 'flow' of returners depicted in Figure 4.5 shows that there is roughly a three to one chance that the returner will go to an institution other than that attended in the first place. Sub-analyses conducted at the level of the six factors given in Chapter 4 showed significant differences at at least the .05 level on three (poor quality of the student experience, unhappiness with the social environment and wrong choice of programme), with those who had switched institutions being more dissatisfied than those who had returned to their original institution. The first of these factors is of clear relevance to insti-tutions and indicates that, for the 'switching' students at least, the quality of the student experience was a determining issue.

Where the same institution was selected, the student was nearly four times as likely to re-enter the same or a similar programme as a different one, though when a new institution was selected the split was close to even. About one-third of the respondents indicated that they saw themselves as not hav-ing to repeat a year's worth of study (though they may have in effect written off their study for a part-year prior to withdrawal and have had to repay the relevant amount of maintenance award). For these students the period of withdrawal is close to being a period of intercalation, with the opportunity for flexibility in attendance being exploited. This is the kind of development that could be affected by changes in the way students are funded in respect of higher education and would need to be incorporated into the modelling of student participation at sectoral level.

Those part-time students who returned to the same institution after a period seem in the main to have been happy with the programme on which they had previously enrolled. On the other hand, roughly a similar number opted for a different institution (and sometimes programme), suggesting that provision at the first institution was felt to be unsatisfactory in some way. There were no significant differences between those who had returned to their original institution and those who had moved elsewhere as far as the six factors given in Chapter 5 were concerned, although there were indications from finer-grained analyses that dissatisfaction with aspects of the student experience was stronger in those who had changed institution. However, the numbers in this analysis were small.

The surveys did not attempt to investigate the rationales for choices sub-sequent to a period of withdrawal, but institutions would probably find such information to be of potential value — but to collect it would require them to attempt to keep in touch with those departing prematurely in a manner similar to the way in which they attempt to keep in touch with alumni. After all, if an institution aims to establish a relationship with each student it enrols, it seems almost perverse to seek to retain that relationship with only those who complete their programmes successfully.

Background characteristics

Age

Full-time and sandwich students who entered higher education aged 21 or above were more likely to report the impact of financial problems, the needs of dependants, the demands of employment whilst studying, emotional difficulties with others, the lack of support from their families (an issue probably not unconnected with emotional difficulties) and travel difficulties. Their under-21 peers, on the other hand, reported more often that they had made the wrong choice of field of study, the programme was not what they had expected, they lacked commitment, the programme was not relevant to their career, they were unhappy with the way the programme was taught and they were unhappy with aspects of the environment in which they were studying. The young students were also more likely to feel that they needed a break from education. One sees in this evidence both the advantages and disadvantages of maturity. If these findings find echoes in the broader body of students, then could it be that some apparently successful students (in that they end up with qualifications) are nevertheless underachieving.

The effect of age on the withdrawal of part-time students is less clear but, for the students aged under 25 on entry, there does seem to be something of an echo of the younger full-time and sandwich withdrawers' lack of commitment to their studies and perceptions of difficulties with their programmes. This may reflect the inadequacy of personal understanding of the nature of the demand of higher education, and possibly hints at the need for greater attention during the admissions process to apprising students of what is to be expected of them.

Gender

For both full-time/sandwich and part-time students, male withdrawers, more than females, tended to report more difficulty with aspects of studying, citing more frequently a lack of study skills and/or commitment, difficulty with the programme and lack of academic progress. For part-time male students, it was noted that they more frequently reported that the programme was not what they had expected and that they were dissatisfied with the quality of the teaching. This gender difference is a matter worthy of further study, and may in part be reflecting the tendency that some have noted for the spread of men's performances to be wider than that of women. The *reasons* for the differences, however, are unclear and are likely to be best elucidated through detailed qualitative study.

As might be expected, there was a greater tendency for older women than for older men (and younger women) to withdraw as a consequence of commitments to nurturing others. However, the older the male student, the more likely it appears that he also will have responsibilities in respect of dependants that trigger withdrawal. Whether this could be countered by policy initiatives (such as extra support) is not clear. Personal experience with the administration of 'Access Funds' suggests that a greater measure of support regarding childcare and the care of other dependants could reduce the chances of withdrawal — but this kind of support often does not come cheap.

Social class

As far as full-time and sandwich students were concerned, working class withdrawers cited significantly more often than others financial difficulty as influencing their decision. In contrast, they cited less frequently dissatisfaction with the social environment and the fact of having made the wrong choice of programme. Age may be playing a part here, in that the distribution of ages showed the group of working class withdrawers to have a higher proportion who were aged over 21 on entry. Further analyses showed that financial difficulty was more likely to discourage working class students from returning to study. The age factor probably accounts to some extent for the greater level of dissatisfaction expressed by the middle/upper class withdrawers. Where part-time students were concerned, middle/upper class withdrawers cited more often than others their dissatisfaction with the quality of the student experience. However, the data only allow one to wonder whether this might be connected with a greater tendency on the part of such people not to put up with a service that they deem to be unsatisfactory.

The qualitative information provided by some respondents also hinted at tensions when they found themselves in groups of a predominantly different class. This is an issue which some academics might not pick up but is one which could be brought to academics' attention when small group teaching is on the agenda of institutional and/or departmental teaching development programmes.

Membership of an ethnic minority group

The number of respondents from ethnic minorities was very small and this base is too slender for any secure conclusions to be drawn. Nevertheless, one finding which might cause institutions to reflect on practice is that black withdrawers tended to report lack of staff support as an influence on their withdrawal. There is also a hint that library provision may be less good for this group, but more would need to be known about the nature and culture of the programme the students were following and what implications, if any, these might have for the provision of educational resources.

Effectiveness and efficiency

The sectoral concern with non-completion relates to the effectiveness and efficiency of the higher education system. Effectiveness broadly refers to the extent that the system is achieving its aims, efficiency to the achievement/cost ratio. These two concepts were addressed, albeit obliquely, in Chapters 6 and 7 which respectively dealt with costs and measurement criteria.

Effectiveness

The full programme (non-)completion rate is a partial index of effectiveness since it makes some attempt to identify the extent to which the aims intended for the system (producing appropriate numbers of doctors and engineers, for example) are being fulfilled. As noted in Chapter 7, a particular difficulty with this as a measure is the time taken to acquire the information, hence a rougher index (the JPIWG, 1994b, census approach) was supported which would give reasonable information in a reasonable time.

However, the discussion in Chapter 7 took a fairly liberal line in respect of performance in that it treated all classification levels of first degrees as successes. A more stringent approach might be preferred by some. Given the fact that the upper second class degree is becoming the modal award in many subjects (HEQC, 1996a), some might wish to tighten the index such that, say, only degrees of second class and above are counted in a measure which seeks to make a statement about the achievement of national aims. To this, the rejoinder might be made that many graduates and diplomates enter jobs for which the skills required are more of the 'personal/transferable' type than of the subject itself — the problem with this argument is that, in general, personal/transferable skills are not well picked up in assessment systems and that evidence of achievements in this area tends to be circumstantial.[17] With respect to some types of programme, then, there may be more of a case for the census-based index than there is for others, where the more general notion of 'graduateness' (HEQC, 1997) is of greater importance.

Another problem with using the census index is that, by its very nature, it cannot take account of the extent to which a student makes suboptimal use of the time spent in higher education. It is highly likely that many students will have found themselves, for various reasons (some of which have already been touched on), to be on a programme not ideally suited to their talents. Lacking any index of non-optimality to set alongside the indexes of non-completion discussed in this report, there is no way in which markers can be set for reducing suboptimality.[18]

Efficiency

If non-completion is costing under the Labour government's revised funding arrangements perhaps £50 million in English higher education, the question arises as to how this amount of money might be minimized, and as a consequence how the efficiency of the sector might be raised. There is potential for improvement at the various levels in the system.

With the advent of HESA data sets, it is now open to institutions to undertake more detailed examinations than were possible here in order to identify those types of student who might be 'lower risks' in respect of non-completion, and to concentrate recruitment on them. Although to do so might be expected to result in a bias towards middle class students with A-levels, the evidence from this study suggests that young students with A-levels (predominantly middle class as well) tend to be less enchanted than others with the choices that they make. Older students, who have a greater amount of life-experience, appear on the evidence collected here to be more satisfied that they have made the right choice of studies. A risk analysis might throw up some surprises.

Improving retention

What can institutions do to improve retention?[19] They can 'play as safe as possible' regarding entry but, as Bourner et al. (1991, p. 105) point out, this could be illiberal, restrictive and discriminating against some of those for whom institutional mission statements declare a welcome. However, 'playing safe' in this way may be seen as running counter to other national objectives — for example, regarding the increase in participation in higher education of people from the lower socio-economic groups. The opening-up of higher education cannot be accomplished without risk of non-completion.

The responses of withdrawers show that aspects of the educational experience are felt by some to have a causal influence on premature departure from higher education. The obvious response is to reiterate proposals such as those in the Dearing Report (NCIHE, 1997) about the improvement of teaching. The problem with proposals to improve teaching has at least two dimensions. The first is the competition for attention that exists between teaching and research, in which the latter retains a commanding lead that is bolstered by the perceived benefit of research in respect of funding and — less directly — by the leverage research exerts on 'league tables' of institutions.[20] The second is the time that is likely to be taken for the proposals to deliver the anticipated benefits.

A more contentious proposal is for institutions to be provided with a proportion of their funding against plans to improve teaching and learning, and for the fulfilment of these plans to be audited in a quality assurance process rather different from that currently in existence or that proposed by the Quality Assurance Agency (QAA, 1998). Continued funding of this improvement-oriented 'teaching and learning quantum' would be conditional on maintaining progress already made and on plans for further enhancement.[21]

The improvement of retention, however, is not simply an issue that has to be addressed by institutions. Students can, through their own actions, contribute to an increase in retention, and policies enacted for the higher education system as a whole are likely also to have an influence. Retention may also be enhanced if advice to prospective students is improved. Table 8.2, which is broadly based on the factors identified in Chapters 4 and 5, summarizes some of the relationships between the topic of possible action and where responsibility for that action might lie. However, it does not purport to deal with all the possibilities that are explicit and implicit in the preceding pages, and by now the reader may well have picked out a number of other potentialities for action.

Table 8.2   An overview of where potential for reducing aspects of non-completion might lie

Factor	System	Institution	Student
Wrong choice of programme	(F)	(F, P)	F, P
Unhappiness with the institutional and geographical environment		(F, to a lesser extent P)	F, P
Poor quality of the student experience		F, P	(F, P)
Dissatisfaction with aspects of institutional provision		F, P	
Inability to cope with the demands of the programme		(F, P)	F, P
Matters related to financial need	(F, P)	(F, some P)	F, P

Key: Main sources of action are unbracketed, secondary sources are bracketed.
    F refers to full-time and sandwich students, P to part-time students.

The appropriateness of the choice of programme resides primarily with intending students. It is up to them to be clear about what they want to study (and *how* they want to study), and to find an appropriate programme. Intending students need to be good at self-analysis and at foraging for information. The institution can help regarding the provision of information by making clear what it is that is on offer. At the level of the higher education system, improvement in the quality of intending students' choices might — for some students — be effected by moving towards a post-qualification applications system.

As with choosing a programme so the choice of an institution is, at root, a matter for the intending student. However, the student does not only choose an institution: he or she chooses a geographical locality as well. Some full-time students in the research were unpleasantly surprised by the environment in which they found themselves living. There is a clear message here that students should find out for themselves a lot more than the information provided in published guides to choosing an institution. On this issue institutions can help through the quality and accuracy of the information that they make available. Part-time students tend to travel to an institution from its hinterland and are generally well aware of the environment in which they will find themselves.

Responsibility for the quality of the student experience resides primarily within institutions since they provide the teaching and other resources that underpin the learning experience. Table 8.1 showed something of the heterogeneity of subject disciplines and hence points to the need for academic organizational units to examine ways in which they could contribute to an improvement in student retention. Not being passive receptors of information, students too have a contribution to make here through their active commitment — one of the corollaries of having made a good choice of programme in the first place.

If dissatisfaction with institutional resources is a significant issue, then a self-aware institution will take steps to rectify the situation. Overloaded workstations and overstretched library resources are fairly easy to identify; rather less so is the possible misperception by intending students of the level of resources actually available.

In the first instance it is up to the student to cope with the demands of the programme: the ability to cope is an obvious correlate of the accuracy with which the student has chosen the programme of study. However, it is also up to institutions to look at ways in which the learning experience can be enhanced — they should resist the temptation to blame the victim for poor performance. This is not an argument for 'dumbing down', but one for improving, where necessary, the professionalism necessary to underpin the facilitation of learning.

Lastly, finance. Students have to organize their (usually limited) finances as best they can. As was noted earlier, some find difficulty in doing this when they leave home for the first time and guidance prior to entry to higher education (as promoted by Shelter, for example) is potentially valuable. Many part-time students are faced with problems stemming from their responsibilities towards others — again, budgeting in advance might help some to come to terms with financial stress. Institutions can and do help out some hard-pressed students through their distribution of 'Access Funds'; in 1998 some part-time students became, for the first time, eligible for this support from this source. The difficulty here is that these funds are far smaller than the demand that is placed upon them and many students' applications cannot be accommodated.[22]

The way in which students are funded by the higher education system has an influence on retention. Recent changes could cut two ways in that student choice regarding entry to higher education might be weighted more heavily by considerations of finance[23] or students might be more subject to panic as the magnitude of indebtedness becomes clear. Evidence is accruing from the 1998 'applications round' that the number of applications from mature students has declined compared with previous years, though it is unclear whether this can be attributed to the requirement to pay tuition fees or to a decline in the pool of potential entrants as a consequence of the efforts to recruit mature students in previous years.

Pascarella and Terenzini (1991), writing of the rather different system in the United States, make some points bearing on a system which is relying on an increased level of student self-investment in higher education. Students' own investment, particularly in prestigious institutions, provides a disincentive against leaving without graduating; scholarships and grants tend to have the greatest beneficial effects on persistence; and part-time employment on campus assists completion (but off-campus employment tends to have an adverse effect). There is evidence from this project and elsewhere that student indebtedness in the United Kingdom is currently having an adverse impact on retention, but this may relate to the particular circumstances under which the student loans scheme is currently being operated rather than to other possible approaches to the financing of students' participation. One aspect of the research that does need to be given consideration by policy makers is the connection that it has found between self-reported social class, withdrawal, financial difficulty and the tendency not to return to study after withdrawal. There is in this finding a suggestion of a vicious circle which is inimical to raising the success level in higher education of students from lower socioeconomic backgrounds.

Conceptually, the government's changes to the funding of students consist of a tinkering with the pre-existing approach. The opportunity was not taken in 1997 to reduce the differentiation between full-time and part-time students through the mechanisms such as that of the 'learning bank' proposed by Robertson (1996). The learning bank approach, in which students are provided with a quantum of funding to which they can add from other sources, has particular implications for the flexibility of student engagement in higher education as, under it, students could choose to spend their learning bank account on full-time or part-time study, or on some combination of the two (indeed, the already blurred distinction between the two would be likely to be further blurred under Robertson's proposals). Under Robertson's approach the concept of non-completion has to be reappraised[24] as students may exercise their option to participate in higher education over a timescale considerably in excess of those typically taken as datum-points, perhaps because they would be interleaving higher education with employment (or vice versa).[25] However, some programmes would seem to have greater potential for flexible study than others. A major policy change, such as the introduction of a learning bank, would have implications for retention — insofar as such a term is meaningful when students can participate more flexibly than is currently allowed by the (slowly eroding) distinction between full-time and part-time study.

Clarifying the picture

At the level of the system as a whole, and for the purposes of modelling student flows and hence funding, the interest is in the probability of students completing the studies for which they have been funded. If institutions have different missions, different subject mixes and different student bodies, then the probability of non-completion will differ from institution to institution (and also at more disaggregated levels, such as that of the ASC).[26] The evidence from this study suggests that there are differences between institutional types[27] and ASCs. It should not be overlooked that the differences within the university sector are, as Scott (1995) has clearly shown, more extensive than is captured by the inclusion in this project of two fairly similar pre-1992 universities and two fairly similar post-1992 universities.

It is probably necessary, for sectoral-level purposes, to do two things. First, a set of categories of cognate institutions should be constructed, though this would need to be a more subtle differentiation than the pre-1992 binary divide.[28] Although hitherto there has, in the United Kingdom, been some resistance to placing this on anything other than an unofficial basis (such as the coming together of the 'Russell Group' of pre-1992 universities or the Coalition of Modern Universities), there is more of a tradition of identifying groups of cognate institutions in the United States.[29] Second, there is a need to develop the HESA coding categories for students' leaving along the lines suggested by this research in order that the information collected by HESA can more closely relate to the real reasons students give for leaving.[30] It then ought to be possible for the system to obtain a clearer picture than it does at present of non-completion and hence to model more accurately its likely effects.

As usual, there are caveats. The first will be familiar by now, in that, if funding is in some way influenced by the reason for withdrawal (dichotomized, say, into institutionally related causes and causes extraneous to the institution), then it is quite likely that this will give rise to some distortion in institutional reporting of data. The second is that, if the 'terms of trade' under which students enter higher education are changed, then this will have an effect on the extent to which different influences impact upon actual withdrawals — the experiences of the past will be unlikely to be an adequate analytical foundation for the evolving future. Third, consumerist 'guides' to higher education will continue to acquire and publish information relating to withdrawal. Institutions can therefore be expected to be somewhat guarded as to the detail of what they release into the public domain for a variety of reasons.

Possibilities for benchmarking

Until comparatively recently there was no strong tradition in the United Kingdom of institutional collection of data regarding student non-completion save at very basic levels. This is in marked contrast to the position in the United States where — as was noted in Chapter 2 — offices of institutional research routinely conduct retention studies for their own institutions and report them publicly at meetings such as the Forums of the Association for Institutional Research. Indeed, it is a commonplace for such gatherings to include the reports of institutional surveys, though synoptic reviews are conspicuously rare.

The situation has changed markedly, for which funding methodologies and the demands of accountability must be given some credit. In response to the growing interest in retention, for example, Napier University has been running a Student Retention Programme since 1995 and has been using withdrawal statistics disaggregated by faculty for the purposes of intra-institutional benchmarking (Johnston and Pollock, 1998). This anticipated by a couple of years the intention of the Scottish Higher Education Funding Council (SHEFC) to identify and visit programmes which had high non-progression rates (see SHEFC, 1997).

In 1996–97 22 English institutions responded to a request to provide, on a confidential basis, 'off the shelf' information about their own investigations into non-completion. These investigations appear to have been differentially successful. One institution had offered entry to a draw for a prize as an inducement to complete its questionnaire but had attracted only a disappointing 16 per cent response rate from those who had withdrawn the previous academic year. At the other end of the scale, another institution (which used a telephone survey for fewer than a hundred leavers) had achieved a response rate of 81 per cent. The modal response percentage from those institutions which had used mailed surveys with relatively recent leavers was of the order of 30 per cent, which is consistent with the published literature. The data from these surveys are not commensurate, which makes it more difficult for institutions (who might wish to share information on a voluntary and confidential basis) to make benchmarking comparisons.

A survey questionnaire such as that developed for this research could be adopted by a group of institutions interested in using comparisons in the interests of improvement. Those working on this research all found that the exercise had been useful to them in their work, but a feature of the collaboration was the mutual trust that was built up by members of the group over a period of time. At a less detailed level, and if developed to give a better indication of the causes of withdrawal, HESA data would also allow comparisons — and would have the advantage of not requiring any extra effort by institutions in respect of data collection. The weakness of using the existing HESA records is that they allow only a single reason for withdrawal when — as this research and other studies have shown — withdrawal very often has more than a single determinant.

Benchmarking is easier to conduct on an intra-institutional basis using data garnered from surveys such as those reported in this book, and inter-institutional sensitivities do not intrude into the process. Comparisons based on the relatively crude differentiation provided by ASCs can be presented in a manner similar to that of Table 8.1 in order to show how the pattern of influences on withdrawal can vary. The point of the exercise is increasing understanding about the reasons for withdrawal so that, where possible, something can be done to reduce it. A curious omission from published work on non-completion and student satisfaction is the bringing of data together in order to produce a comprehensive picture of the relationship between the two. One might pick up early warnings from the student satisfaction surveys that would allow action to be taken to reduce the possibility that dissatisfaction would be converted into withdrawal.

The funding of institutions with reference to non-completion

Whatever the nature of the higher education system in the post-Dearing era, it is clear that higher education in England has undergone a considerable shift over the past two decades. The optimal point of balance between enrolment and non-completion has moved from a position of narrow/low to one which can probably be characterized as relatively broad/relatively higher. The difficulty is that there is as yet no consensus on what the magnitude of 'relatively higher' should be. Clearly, the basis of judgement should not be that of a bygone age.

Should the funding of institutions take into account withdrawal statistics? The question was answered partially in Chapter 7, and three responses are made here.

1. The first response relates to the aims set for the higher education system. If widening access is desired, then it would be unfair to penalize institutions which have responded to this challenge by opening their doors to all (or, perhaps more likely, the majority) of those who might benefit from it. Institutional mission, and practical commitment to that mission, would need to be taken into account — which would require judgements to be made about the relationship of mission to national expectation.

2. Even if the technical inadequacies in the indexes suggested in Chapter 7 are overlooked, the inclusion of non-completion data would be likely to have an effect on institutional behaviour. This might be positive in that an improvement in the quality of teaching might be stimulated, or adverse in that institutions might be tempted to minimize failures. Regarding the former, suggestions were made earlier that might have a more direct effect on teaching. Regarding academic failure, the pressures on the external examining system (Silver, 1995; HEQC, 1996c) make it doubtful that many external examiners would be in a position to identify whether the boundary of failure was being eased downwards (this would apply particularly at intermediate stages in bachelor's degree programmes). The net result could be a lowering of standards. The proposals put forward by the Quality Assurance Agency (QAA, 1998) for a system of Registered External Examiners are unlikely to be able to deal adequately with the issue.

3. The third response is grounded in the empirical data presented in Chapters 4 and 5. The factor analyses suggested six factors underlying

the withdrawal of full-time and sandwich students, and also six (slightly different in composition) for that of part-time students. Some factors, such as student satisfaction with the learning experience or the provision of facilities, may have their origin in matters which are under institutional control, although the relationship between the perceptions of the students and those of the institution (and also those of an objective observer) is of course problematic. Other factors, such as problems of a personal nature, the actual location of the institution and (to a large extent) financial problems, seem to lie outside the capacity of the institution to rectify.

A third group of factors appears to have ambiguous loci of control. The choice of field of study may be that of the student, but that choice will often be influenced by what the institution appears to be placing on offer through prospectuses, open days and so on. Thirty-seven per cent of the full-time and sandwich respondents reported that their programme was not what they had expected. As noted in Chapter 4, the percentage was highest in the pre-1992 universities and was also higher in students who commenced their programmes when they were under 21. The causes of the problem can probably be attributed to both students and the institutions at either end of the transition between school and higher education, but there is no evidence as to where the greater responsibility might lie. If the student does not understand, after the application and admissions process, what the programme expects of him or her, then — again — this could be the result of a failure on the part of student or institution, or both.

On this analysis, it seems difficult to see how institutional non-completion statistics can accurately be brought to bear on institutional funding. Institutions differ in the weightings that they give different national objectives, and this difference is likely to be reflected in their non-completion rates. A connection between funding and non-completion could have an adverse effect on standards. Finally, it will be difficult — if not impossible — to partition out that component of non-completion that can be attributed to institutional performance.

It should, of course, be recalled from Chapter 7 that non-completion does find its way into the existing HEFCE funding methodology as institutions do not receive their core funding for a full-time or sandwich student unless he or she remains at the institution until the end of the funding year in question.

The relationship of the findings to Tinto's model

Of those who have attempted to theorize withdrawal, Tinto (1993) has adopted the most wide-ranging approach. It seems appropriate, therefore, to explore how the findings from this research fit in with the model that Tinto derived from his theorizing.

The 'fit' of this research to Tinto's theorizing

In general terms, Tinto's model appears to provide a better fit with the data from part-time students than with those from full-time and sandwich students because the part-time students are more obviously in a position to apply the calculus of advantage in respect of competing demands on their attention. In the fact that 52 per cent of the part-time respondents identified the demands of employment as at least moderately influential in the decision to withdraw, one sees the salience and determining potential of those components of the model that deal with intentions, goals, institutional commitments and external commitments. For full-time and sandwich students, the evidence from the study hints at some shift of salience towards those components that deal with the experience within higher education itself.

It will be recalled that Tinto's longitudinal model of institutional departure related pre-entry requirements, initial goals and commitments, institutional experiences, academic and social integration into higher education, and adjusted goals and commitments to departure from the institution. For Tinto, writing about non-completion in the context of the United States, financial considerations are not of primary importance because these are typically taken into account by students at the time when entry is being contemplated. Although they may stand proxy for some form of calculation of the benefit/cost ratio relating to continuation,[31] Tinto's model omits this aspect of withdrawal (unless it is buried in the re-identification of intentions and goals during the programme), perhaps because it is difficult to locate along the dimension of time. From the perspective of current higher education in the United Kingdom, in which some students have only appreciated the financial implications of entering higher education after they have entered, this omission has to be considered a weakness. However, given that the government of the United Kingdom has decided that students will pay a part of their tuition fee 'up front', Tinto's placing of financial support at the pre-entry stage may be more relevant as the millennium approaches.

Tinto's model, though it refers to intentions and to goal and institutional commitments, also appears to deal inadequately with the *choice* of programme of study. The findings of this survey — as of others[32] — show that this is the influence on withdrawal that is most frequently reported by students who entered full-time or sandwich programmes at an age lower than 21 (most of these will in practice be school leavers). There is a clear potential for wrong choice to lead into a downward spiral of decreased motivation and lowered performance. A hint of this is contained in the connection between wrong choice and commitment noted earlier.

Higher education in the United Kingdom, particularly for the younger full-time and sandwich students, is often characterized by study in an institution geographically distinct from the student's home town. Although dislike of the geographical location is not very often mentioned as having influenced withdrawal (15 per cent of the full-time and sandwich students reported dislike of the city/town and 10 per cent feared crime), it is clear that, for some students, environmental factors do have a bearing on why they persist or leave. To some extent this is taken into account by Tinto in his reference to social integration, but studying at what is perceived to be a considerable distance from home may be of less significance in the United States where the community colleges have traditionally been a key component of the higher education system.[33]

One can also can take issue with Tinto regarding the lack, in his model, of a personal health dimension. Twenty-three per cent of full-time and sandwich withdrawers reported health problems as influential on their decision to withdraw, and 7 per cent reported that drugs or alcohol had had an influence. Perhaps slightly surprisingly, although the percentage of withdrawers citing stress related to the programme as an influence was almost identical to that citing health problems, the statistical association between the two influences was only weak.

Issues of personal well-being seem to be given little, if any, attention in Tinto's conceptualization of departure in terms of academic performance, interpersonal interactions of various kinds, and academic and social integration.[34] However, even if some of the influences that relate to the academic and social systems are partialled out, there remain an indeterminate number of students for whom health problems have had serious implications for completion of their programmes of study. Particularly sadly, as was found in a small number of instances, the cause of non-completion was death. As with financial problems, health does not fit neatly into a diachronic model since problems can strike at any time.

Lastly, it can be argued that Tinto's theorizing has comparatively little to say about students' experiences of teaching and learning. This may be a consequence of his sociological perspective. His interest in rites of passage, following Van Gennep's work,[35] appears to have led him to stress the importance of induction (beginning classrooms being seen as gateways) over educational processes in the longer term. True, there are references to the fact that large lectures stifle contact with lecturers (Tinto, 1993, p. 119), but broader dimensions of students' satisfaction with their experiences are given little discussion. It seems that they are being swept up in the area of his model that encompasses academic performance, faculty/staff interactions and academic integration. More recently Tinto (1997) has given greater attention to issues of educational process in a study of curriculum implementation at Seattle Community College. In this study he provides evidence to the positive effect of clustering study units, which gives students more of an 'academic home' than the more open-choice curriculum that had been the College's norm.

The evidence from the research reported in this book indicates that the dimensions of student satisfaction are of importance, and implies that these have an influence on the motivation/performance interrelationship noted earlier.

An explanatory theory?

Tinto has, for a couple of decades, been seeking to develop an explanatory theory of students' premature departure from higher education. If one makes adjustments along the lines suggested in the previous section, it is possible to see — looking back on student non-completion — how, for each student, a particular congeries of circumstances may have triggered withdrawal. From the point of the theory's practical utility, however, rather more is needed. The policy maker at the level of the system needs to know how much weight to place on the various possible causes, as do those responsible (in their various ways) for the progression of students through an institution.

To what extent can Tinto's theory (adapted as necessary) be said to be *predictive* of student withdrawal and suggestive of means through which withdrawal can be minimized? For those concerned with the overall performance of the higher education system, the theory will probably prove to be of limited use since many of the components of Tinto's model will be unknown at the level of the system. Whereas there will be some general — if limited — knowledge about students' background characteristics, those aspects of the model that relate to intentions and goals, and to the academic and social aspects of participation, will be obscure. The system's monitoring will only track the continuation of the student in higher education and his or her ultimate departure. Much that is important to non-completion will take place in a 'black box' into which 'the system' will have limited access. At the level of the institution, things are a little better. The institution (or, at least, its components) will have access to some of the information in the black box of process in that there will be knowledge of performances and some understanding of the student's personality, circumstances, aims and general engagement. The problems are that the information is likely to be dispersed amongst a number of individuals and that some of the relevant information (for example, commitments outside the institution) will not be known. On this basis, prediction is likely to be hazardous unless some powerfully precipitating factor is apparent.

Many have pointed out the array of factors that can underlie non-completion in which variables interact in complex ways. At some point, a critical moment is passed at which a preparedness to continue is converted into a decision to discontinue — or possibly a 'non-decision' simply to drift away (Stowell, 1998). Many in higher education will no doubt be able to point to a pair of students in broadly similar circumstances, one of whom perseveres against quite substantial odds whereas the other discontinues. McGivney (1996), generalizing the point with reference to mature students, writes '. . . while outside pressures of work and family prove too great for some mature students, many others manage to overcome similar pressures' (p. 111). The number of academic, personal, social and economic variables that bear on the decision is generally too great for prediction to be undertaken with confidence. Tinto's theorizing may at best help the estimation of probabilities (and should not be disparaged for that, since it provides a reminder of what needs to be taken into account), but is formulated at too general a level for anything approaching accurate prediction.

Coda: the empirical deficit revisited

A substantial longitudinal study is already being undertaken by HEFCE, which is interrogating national student records in order to establish the movement of students through the system. As students do not use unique identifiers (such as Social Security numbers), the tracking of the students has to be done by matching a number of fields from the records. This work is likely to give a more accurate picture of non-completion, since the institutionally based records used hitherto tend to be blind to student movement to other institutions — and occasionally to intra-institutional movement.

Data relating to student non-completion are 'noisy'. There are general trends to be detected, such as those identified in Table 8.1, but these are per-fused by a variety of factors which, individually and severally, are idiosyncratic. Studies on a substantial scale are needed in order to identify the main signals from amongst the cacophony of individuals' experiences.

The work described in this book constitutes a modest contribution to reducing the empirical deficit. Higher education, however, is in a period of rapid change and hence there is a need for such work to be replicated over a number of years in order to determine whether the main causes of non-completion are changing in tandem. Such a series of still pictures can be made to approximate a movie film, even if rather jerkily.

'Autopsy' studies of non-completion still leave open the question of whether what students say after withdrawal is a reasonable representation of the cause(s) of that withdrawal. In the research described in this book it was necessary to make the pragmatic assumption that what the students said about their non-completion was true, though there is an indeterminate possibility that the assumption does not hold. Autopsy studies tell little of the way in which non-completion is precipitated. Given the relative lack of understanding of the causality of non-completion, there is a strong case for following a substantial cohort of students through higher education in order better to identify, through longitudinal study, how it is that students end up in a position such that withdrawal or exclusion takes place. The findings could be expected to lead to greater effectiveness in attempts to minimize non-completion. Given the estimated costs of non-completion, research along these lines ought to have a compelling relationship between cost and benefit.

Notes

1. See, for example, Woodley et al. (1987, pp. 162–3).
2. It was argued in Chapter 6 that the true figures may be double.

3. A 'nested levels' approach to performance indicators has been suggested by Yorke (1996b) which, whilst underplaying the complex interrelationships between levels of the higher education system, provides a heuristic for discussion.
4. McGivney (1996), though writing about mature students, provides a useful overview of the general position.
5. It would have to be accepted that 'placement in higher education' as an indicator of school performance would have to be modified to take into account delayed entry.
6. Some examples could not be quoted in this book because they would lead to the identification of the institutions involved.
7. Using dichotomized data for these two variables, the phi coefficient was 0.35 ($p = .0000$) for the respondents as a whole ($N = 2146$).
8. It was noted earlier that the intending students themselves and careers advisers also have responsibility for obtaining the best match.
9. See Kingston (1998) for a critical article on prospectuses and Robertson (1994, paras 882–5) for proposals aimed at improving them.
10. Higgins (1998) suggests that school students in general know much better what they want to do when they have completed two years of study at Advanced level and when the A-level results are published.
11. It has to be remembered that, for this ASC, the number of respondents was only 15.
12. Three ASCs were noticeably different from the rest as far as the distribution of respondents' ages was concerned: ASC 2, ASC 8 and ASC 11. Each of the three had around 25 per cent of respondents of the age of 25 and above, but ASC 11 (11 per cent) had the highest proportion of students aged 35 and above.
13. They have, in addition, been less able to draw benefits from the state — for example, they are no longer allowed to draw unemployment benefit during the vacations.
14. HEQC (1995, 1996b).
15. For a policy-oriented discussion of some of the issues, see Yorke, McCormick and Chapman (1996).
16. See, for instance, Ramsden (1992).
17. See, on the issue of bringing personal/transferable skills more to the fore in assessment, Yorke (1996a). To use an index of this sort would, however, leave third class and unclassified degrees in a limbo between failure and success.
18. Robertson (1994) discusses a number of points relevant to the reduction of suboptimality at various places in his Chapter XIII.
19. There is a great deal that can be said here, but to do so would take this volume away from its primary purpose. For those who need a fuller account, McGivney (1996), pp. 120–66 covers a lot of the ground.
20. See Yorke (1997a, 1998b) for analyses that demonstrate the dominance of research in *The Times'* league tables of 1996 and 1997.
21. See Yorke (1996c).
22. 'Access funds' are made available through institutions and are available to part-time students taking 60 credits as well as to full-time and sandwich students. However, fairness in distribution is difficult to achieve — and higher education institutions are not (nor should they be) equipped to assess personal finances with the rigour of a tax office or a credit-rating agency. Institutions also have their own hardship funds which can be called upon in cases of urgent need.

23. Tuition fee payments are means-tested, with the least well-off not being required to pay. Whether this will be sufficient to encourage the participation of those with weak financial backgrounds remains to be seen.
24. It would probably have to be approached, both definitially and in terms of performance indicators, from the perspective of the completion of the study unit.
25. If students can be funded with flexibility of participation in mind, then the same principle can be adopted with institutions. There seems no reason why institutional core funding could not be provided on a 'student credit' basis rather than on the block basis that is currently used. Information systems now have the power to handle data at this level of detail.
26. The significance of institutional diversity for the use of performance indicators is recognized by HEFCE, for instance in its circular letter 20/98 (HEFCE, 1998).
27. There are also differences within types as in this research the two institutions coalesced under the heading of 'colleges' are in practice very different in character.
28. And would need to recognize the position of institutions such as the specialist monotechnics, for example.
29. The Integrated Postsecondary Education Data System (IPEDS) database run by the National Center for Educational Statistics has provided a basis for institutions to identify other similar institutions for various benchmarking purposes.
30. The potential for difference between the stated and true reasons for withdrawal is acknowledged; however, for practical purposes the stated reasons may be as close to the truth as one can get.
31. Tinto (1993, p. 88).
32. See, for example, Moore's work quoted in McGivney (1996, p. 108).
33. This is more developed than the franchising and associated college networks established in recent years in the United Kingdom. Changes in the funding of higher education, and possibly in its structure and its relationship with further education, could, however, change this position quite markedly.
34. To be fair, Tinto does acknowledge the power of external forces (see, for example, Tinto, 1993, p. 109) — but his remarks are dominated by sociological rather than other forces.
35. See Tinto (1993, pp. 94ff.).

List of Appendices

Appendix 1 Some background information relating to the respondents
      (a)   Full-time and sandwich students
      (b)   Part-time students

Appendix 2 Comparisons of responses

Appendix 3 Outcomes of factor analyses
      (a)   Full-time and sandwich students
      (b)   Part-time students

Appendix 4 Selected comparisons for both full-time and sandwich students and part-time students

Only those comparisons which showed significant differences are included. This should not be interpreted as implying that other data are of little interest since important influences on withdrawal may be common to various groups in the analyses. Refer back to Tables 4.2 and 5.1 for the general level of responses.

    (a)   (i)   Comparison by Academic Subject Category (full-time and sandwich students only)
          (ii)   Bonferroni *post hoc* comparisons between ASCs
    (b)   Comparison by Academic Subject Category (part-time students only)
    (c)   (i)   Comparison by age (full-time and sandwich students only)
          (ii)   Comparison by age (part-time students only)
    (d)   Comparison by Clearing (full-time and sandwich students only)
    (e)   (i)   Comparison by gender (full-time and sandwich students only)
          (ii)   Comparison by gender (part-time students only)
    (f)   Comparison by type of institution (full-time and sandwich students only)
    (g)   (i)   Comparison by level of programme (full-time and sandwich students only)

(ii) Comparison by level of programme (part-time students only)

(h) Comparison by match of entry qualifications to programme (full-time and sandwich students only)

(i) Comparison by number of subjects in the programme (full-time and sandwich students only)

(j) (i) Comparison by social class (full-time and sandwich students only)

(ii) Comparison by social class (part-time students only)

Appendix 1: Some Background Information Relating to the Respondents

(a) Full-time and sandwich students (N = 2151)

Gender:
Male	1026
Female	1118
Not given	7

Age on entry:
Under 21	1438
21 and over	699
Not given	14

Social class (self-reported):
Working class	490
'No particular class'	518
Middle/upper class	576
Not given/not asked	567

Ethnicity:
White	1458
Black	19
Asian	81
Other	20
Not given/not asked	573

Disability:
With disability	117
Not with disability	1487
Not given/not asked	547

Percentage having entered higher education on the basis of A-levels, by institutional type:

Pre-1992 university	72
Post-1992 university	56
Colleges	60

Type of programme taken:

Single subject	1110
Two or more subjects	845
Not given	196

Level of programme taken:

Degree level	1828
Sub-degree level	213
Not given	110

Academic Subject Category of programme taken, by institutional type:

ASC	Subjects subsumed	Pre-1992 university	Post-1992 university	College	Total
1	Clinical and Pre-Clinical	15	0	0	15
2	Subjects and Professions Allied to Medicine	17	75	11	103
3	Science	91	143	30	264
4	Engineering and Technology	75	67	53	195
5	Built Environment	20	44	4	68
6	Mathematics, IT and Computing	32	71	23	126
7	Business and Management	16	190	27	233
8	Social Science	55	132	32	219
9	Humanities	103	128	55	286
10	Art, Design and Performing Arts	9	83	12	104
11	Education	0	118	3	121
50	Mixed Arts-based	32	46	14	92
51	Mixed Science-based	10	27	19	56
52	Mixed Arts-based and Science-based	19	46	17	82
				Total	**1964**
				Not given	187

(b) Part-time students (N = 328)

Gender:

Male	114
Female	211
Not given	3

Age on entry:

Under 25	62
25 and over	262
Not given	4

Social class (self-reported):
Working class	100
'No particular class'	114
Middle/upper class	104
Not given	10

Ethnicity:
White	297
Black	10
Asian	8
Other	3
Not given/not asked	10

Disability:
With disability	30
Not with disability	291
Not given	7

Type of programme taken:
Single subject	146
Two or more subjects	77
Not given	105

Level of programme taken:
Degree level	207
Sub-degree level	105
Not given	16

Academic Subject Category of programme taken, by institutional type:

ASC	Subjects subsumed	Pre-1992 university	Post-1992 university	College	Total
1	Clinical and Pre-Clinical	0	0	0	0
2	Subjects and Professions Allied to Medicine	3	64	9	76
3	Science	0	8	0	8
4	Engineering and Technology	0	8	4	12
5	Built Environment	0	10	3	13
6	Mathematics, IT and Computing	2	9	0	11
7	Business and Management	0	78	12	90
8	Social Science	2	40	2	44
9	Humanities	3	12	4	19
10	Art, Design and Performing Arts	0	0	1	1
11	Education	2	19	0	21
50	Mixed Arts-based	0	1	0	1
51	Mixed Science-based	1	2	0	3
52	Mixed Arts-based and Science-based	2	0	0	2
	Total	**15**	**251**	**35**	**301**
				Not given	27

Appendix 2: Comparison of Responses

Comparison of the responses from the mail and telephone surveys of students withdrawing in, or at the end of, academic year 1994–5

Variable	Mean Percentage Mail survey	Phone survey	Chi-square	Signif. of difference
Inadequate staff support outside timetable	23	33	17.41	.0000
Accommodation problems	17	19	.29	ns
Insufficient academic progress	31	44	24.14	.0000
Lack of commitment to programme	33	51	44.25	.0000
Institutional computing provision	08	14	13.06	.0003
Demands of employment whilst studying	14	20	9.75	.0018
Needs of dependants	16	15	.03	ns
Problems with drugs/alcohol	07	07	.00	ns
Emotional difficulties with others	25	19	5.66	ns
Lack of personal support from family	12	11	.19	ns
Fear of crime	09	11	.51	ns
Financial problems	36	43	7.34	.0067
Difficulty in making friends	09	07	.60	ns
Dislike of city/town	16	15	.26	ns
Health problems	22	25	1.07	ns
Homesickness	11	11	.09	ns
Institution not as expected	17	20	1.26	ns
Institutional library provision	07	12	9.82	.0017
Class size too large	15	24	18.87	.0000
Needed a break from education	25	39	31.02	.0000
Programme not as expected	34	44	12.99	.0003
Difficulty of the programme	18	31	29.38	.0000
Organization of the programme	25	34	13.49	.0002
Quality of the teaching	21	31	18.02	.0000
Programme not relevant to career	17	35	57.14	.0000
Institutional provision of social facilities	07	13	14.78	.0001
Lack of study skills	15	25	22.56	0000
Institutional provision of specialist equipment	06	12	16.86	.0000
Lack of personal support from staff	25	28	1.43	ns
Stress related to the programme	20	27	8.77	.0031
Lack of personal support from students	14	16	1.45	ns
Timetabling did not suit	09	15	8.80	.0031
Travel difficulties	14	15	.39	ns
Way the programme was taught did not suit	28	42	29.50	.0000
Chose wrong field of study	36	48	20.53	.0000
Workload too heavy	15	25	19.80	.0000

Appendix 3: Outcomes of Factor Analyses

(a) Full-time and sandwich students

Possible influence	Percentage of the variance:	Factor					
		1 19.6	2 8.0	3 6.6	4 5.9	5 4.6	6 3.8
Quality of the teaching		.80					
Inadequate staff support outside timetable		.77					
Organization of the programme		.77					
Way programme was taught did not suit		.76					
Lack of personal support from staff		.67					
Class size too large		.55					
Timetabling did not suit		.40					
Stress related to the programme			.71				
Difficulty of the programme			.67				
Workload too heavy			.67				
Lack of study skills			.57				
Lack of personal support from students			.45				
Insufficient academic progress		.33	.45		.41		
Dislike of city/town				.72		.35	
Homesickness				.71			
Fear of crime				.62			
Difficulty in making friends				.60			
Accommodation problems				.58			
Chose wrong field of study					.75		
Programme not relevant to career					.71		
Lack of commitment to programme					.69		
Programme not as expected		.48			.53		
Needed a break from education					.39		
Financial problems						.71	
Demands of employment whilst studying						.65	
Lack of personal support from family						.54	
Needs of dependants						.48	
Travel difficulties						.48	
Emotional difficulties with others						.44	

continued . . .

Quality *Possible influence*	*Percentage of the variance:*	*1* *19.6*	*2* *8.0*	*3* *6.6*	*4* *5.9*	*5* *4.6*	*6* *3.8*
				Factor			

Quality *Possible influence*		1	2	3	4	5	6
Institutional library provision							.79
Institutional computing provision							.74
Institutional provision of specialist equipment							.69
Institutional provision of social facilities							.64
Institution not as expected		.38		.38			.42
Health problems							
Problems with drugs/alcohol							

Factor analysis of 2151 full-time and sandwich respondents' reporting of influences on their withdrawal. Loadings of I .30 I and above shown, for clarity: two variables did not load on the factors at this criterion level.

The Kaiser-Meyer-Olkin measure of sampling adequacy was .87.

(b) Part-time students

		Factor					
Possible influence	Percentage of the variance:	1 17.3	2 8.1	3 7.3	4 5.6	5 4.9	6 4.6
Inadequate staff support outside timetable		.80					
Lack of personal support from staff		.78			.34		
Organization of the programme		.76					
Quality of the teaching		.75					
Way programme was taught did not suit		.72					
Class size too large		.59					
Lack of personal support from students		.58					
Programme not as expected		.55					.49
Insufficient academic progress		.49					
Institution not as expected		.45		.32			
Workload too heavy			.75				
Demands of employment whilst studying			.66				
Stress related to the programme			.62				
Timetabling did not suit			.54				
Programme difficulty		.31	.39				
Needed a break from education			.37		.36		
Travel difficulties			.33			.31	
Dislike of city/town				.87			
Homesickness				.78			
Fear of crime				.78			
Accommodation problems				.64			
Lack of personal support from family					.72		
Emotional difficulties with others					.69		
Needs of dependants					.50		
Financial problems					.46		
Difficulty in making friends					.38	.31	
Health problems					.34		
Institutional provision of social facilities						.69	
Institutional computing provision		.31				.64	
Institutional provision of specialist equipment						.59	
Institutional library provision						.57	
Chose wrong field of study							.74
Programme not relevant to career							.66
Lack of commitment to programme			.41				.45
Lack of study skills							
Problems with drugs/alcohol							

Factor analysis of 328 part-time respondents' reporting of influences on their withdrawal. Loadings of | .30 | and above shown, for clarity: two variables did not load on to the factors at this criterion level.

The Kaiser-Meyer-Olkin measure of sampling adequacy is 0.77.

Appendix 4: Selected Comparisons for both Full-time and Sandwich Students and Part-time Students

(a) (i) Comparison by Academic Subject Category (full-time and sandwich students only)

Variable	Component of factor no.	1 N=15 Mean	2 N=103 Mean	3 N=264 Mean	4 N=195 Mean	5 N=68 Mean	6 N=126 Mean	7 N=233 Mean	8 N=219 Mean	9 N=286 Mean	10 N=104 Mean	11 N=121 Mean	50 N=92 Mean	51 N=56 Mean	52 N=82 Mean	F	p
Factor 1	1	0.06	-0.01	-0.03	0.18	0.03	0.01	0.09	-0.14	-0.18	0.43	-0.15	0.13	-0.06	0.13	3.63	0.0000
Factor 2	1	0.94	-0.02	0.10	0.28	0.09	0.04	-0.16	0.02	0.01	-0.22	-0.11	-0.15	0.26	-0.18	4.08	0.0000
Factor 3	1	-0.18	-0.08	0.03	-0.07	-0.04	-0.37	-0.02	0.12	0.18	0.14	-0.05	0.17	-0.18	-0.07	3.07	0.0002
Factor 4	1	-0.09	-0.28	0.14	0.19	0.08	0.14	0.12	-0.23	0.01	-0.13	-0.17	-0.13	0.26	0.21	3.97	0.0000
Factor 5	1	-0.51	-0.02	0.09	-0.04	0.08	-0.09	0.02	0.10	-0.12	-0.12	-0.11	0.02	-0.09	0.14	1.49	ns
Factor 6	1	-0.48	-0.09	0.01	0.09	-0.09	-0.05	0.08	-0.17	-0.03	0.16	-0.08	0.05	0.34	-0.01	1.92	ns
																Chi square	p
Quality of the teaching	1	0.13	0.19	0.22	0.29	0.30	0.24	0.27	0.17	0.15	0.39	0.15	0.29	0.27	0.26	47.82	0.0000
Organization of the programme	1	0.40	0.23	0.25	0.30	0.24	0.24	0.29	0.21	0.19	0.47	0.28	0.34	0.32	0.32	42.28	0.0001
Teaching did not suit me	1	0.40	0.25	0.27	0.41	0.34	0.30	0.36	0.24	0.26	0.47	0.21	0.33	0.32	0.35	42.36	0.0001
Class size too large	1	0.00	0.13	0.23	0.24	0.16	0.17	0.18	0.18	0.10	0.17	0.08	0.14	0.20	0.12	38.32	0.0003
Stress related to the programme	2	0.53	0.23	0.25	0.30	0.24	0.19	0.18	0.20	0.21	0.24	0.21	0.22	0.36	0.16	27.71	0.0099
Difficulty of the programme	2	0.40	0.17	0.28	0.38	0.13	0.31	0.22	0.17	0.14	0.15	0.12	0.16	0.25	0.23	75.78	0.0000
Workload too heavy	2	0.47	0.23	0.19	0.25	0.27	0.17	0.19	0.15	0.13	0.10	0.18	0.09	0.21	0.20	38.46	0.0002
Lack of study skills	2	0.20	0.09	0.21	0.31	0.15	0.22	0.14	0.17	0.12	0.15	0.14	0.16	0.20	0.13	45.30	0.0000
Insufficient academic progress	2	0.47	0.18	0.34	0.45	0.39	0.29	0.30	0.28	0.30	0.38	0.19	0.25	0.39	0.24	46.74	0.0000
Accommodation problems	3	0.07	0.08	0.22	0.18	0.19	0.10	0.19	0.23	0.22	0.24	0.07	0.21	0.12	0.15	37.68	0.0003
Chose wrong field of study	4	0.47	0.32	0.48	0.42	0.43	0.39	0.42	0.31	0.39	0.26	0.41	0.33	0.54	0.44	32.81	0.0018
Lack of commitment to programme	4	0.47	0.25	0.44	0.45	0.40	0.41	0.41	0.36	0.41	0.30	0.22	0.30	0.39	0.45	36.17	0.0003
Programme not as expected	4	0.47	0.39	0.37	0.41	0.33	0.40	0.40	0.27	0.34	0.48	0.27	0.32	0.45	0.50	32.46	0.0021
Financial problems	5	0.07	0.28	0.45	0.39	0.36	0.39	0.34	0.37	0.33	0.44	0.27	0.36	0.39	0.41	28.54	0.0076
Needs of dependants	5	0.13	0.18	0.12	0.10	0.09	0.13	0.17	0.20	0.14	0.10	0.29	0.13	0.11	0.17	38.42	0.0003
Institutional computing provision	6	0.00	0.08	0.08	0.11	0.12	0.12	0.16	0.05	0.06	0.11	0.02	0.10	0.18	0.07	37.63	0.0003
Institutional provision of specialist equipment	6	0.07	0.02	0.07	0.13	0.09	0.07	0.09	0.02	0.06	0.16	0.03	0.07	0.14	0.07	44.64	0.0000
Health problems		0.33	0.29	0.25	0.16	0.24	0.13	0.16	0.25	0.29	0.27	0.15	0.29	0.34	0.18	40.84	0.0001

Note: The Academic Subject Categories are identified on page 37.

135

(a)(ii) Bonferroni *post hoc* comparisons between ASCs

The table below gives Bonferroni *post hoc* comparisons between ASCs (full-time and sandwich students only). 'Scoring higher (lower)' means that the influence of the factor on withdrawal was greater (lesser).

Factor (brief label)	Significant differences	
1 (Student experience)	ASC 10	scoring higher than ASCs 3, 8, 9, 11
	ASC 4	scoring higher than ASC 9
2 (Inability to cope)	ASC 1	scoring higher than ASCs 2, 7, 9, 10, 11, 50, 52
	ASC 4	scoring higher than ASCs 7, 10, 52
3 (Social environment)	ASC 6	scoring lower than ASCs 3, 8, 9, 10, 50
4 (Wrong choice)	ASC 2	scoring lower than ASCs 3, 4
	ASC 8	scoring lower than ASCs 3, 4, 7

(b) Comparison by Academic Subject Category (part-time students only)

Variable		ASC 2 N=76 Mean	ASC 7 N=90 Mean	ASC 8 N=44 Mean	F	p	Sig diff groups
Factor 1		0.02	0.06	0.10	0.10	ns	
Factor 2		0.10	-0.06	0.00	0.45	ns	
Factor 3		-0.17	0.06	0.42	3.23	0.0420	ASC2 v. ASC8
Factor 4		-0.02	-0.05	0.04	0.11	ns	
Factor 5		-0.08	-0.15	0.24	3.13	0.0460	ASC7 v. ASC8
Factor 6		0.05	0.09	-0.29	2.22	ns	
	Component of factor no.				*Chi square*	*p*	
Health problems	4	0.11	0.16	0.30	7.40	0.0248	
Institutional library provision	5	0.13	0.04	0.25	12.08	0.0024	

Note: The Academic Subject Categories are identified on page 37.

(c)(i) Comparison by age (full-time and sandwich students only)

Variable	Component of factor no.	Under 21 N=1438 Mean	21+ N=699 Mean	t	p
Factor 1		0.03	-0.06	-1.86	ns
Factor 2		0.01	0.01	0.20	ns
Factor 3		0.12	-0.25	-8.75	0.0000
Factor 4		0.21	-0.42	-14.46	0.0000
Factor 5		-0.15	0.31	9.53	0.0000
Factor 6		-0.01	0.02	0.54	ns
				Chi square	p
Teaching did not suit me	1	0.33	0.25	15.17	0.0001
Timetabling did not suit	1	0.10	0.14	7.90	0.0049
Difficulty of the programme	2	0.23	0.17	8.87	0.0029
Lack of study skills	2	0.18	0.13	7.88	0.0050
Insufficient academic progress	2	0.33	0.23	23.47	0.0000
Dislike of city/town	3	0.18	0.08	33.47	0.0000
Homesickness	3	0.14	0.05	37.01	0.0000
Fear of crime	3	0.12	0.06	13.11	0.0003
Accommodation problems	3	0.20	0.13	15.88	0.0001
Chose wrong field of study	4	0.47	0.23	110.92	0.0000
Programme not relevant to career	4	0.27	0.15	37.28	0.0000
Lack of commitment to programme	4	0.44	0.24	82.59	0.0000
Needed a break from education	4	0.33	0.19	45.31	0.0000
Financial problems	5	0.33	0.46	36.39	0.0000
Demands of employment whilst studying	5	0.12	0.20	22.33	0.0000
Lack of personal support from family	5	0.09	0.18	35.87	0.0000
Needs of dependants	5	0.09	0.28	123.91	0.0000
Emotional difficulties with others	5	0.22	0.27	7.91	0.0049
Travel difficulties	5	0.13	0.20	17.61	0.0000
Institution not as expected	6	0.21	0.14	12.95	0.0003
Health problems	–	0.21	0.27	8.12	0.0044

(c)(ii) Comparison by age (part-time students only)

Variable	Under 25 N=62 Mean	25+ N=262 Mean	t	p
Factor 1	0.18	−0.04	1.47	ns
Factor 2	0.03	−0.01	0.24	ns
Factor 3	0.32	−0.07	1.53	ns
Factor 4	0.16	−0.05	1.51	ns
Factor 5	0.06	−0.01	0.50	ns
Factor 6	0.23	−0.05	1.84	ns
			Chi square	p
Stress related to the programme	Component of factor no. 2	0.31	0.13	9.58	0.0020
Institutional library provision	5	0.02	0.13	5.32	0.0211

(d) Comparison by Clearing (full-time and sandwich students only)

Variable	Component of factor no.	Not Clearing N=1518 Mean	Clearing N=520 Mean	t	p
Factor 1		-0.03	0.11	-2.62	0.009
Factor 2		0.01	0.01	0.07	ns
Factor 3		0.00	0.02	-0.43	ns
Factor 4		-0.01	0.09	-1.88	ns
Factor 5		-0.04	0.11	-2.95	0.003
Factor 6		-0.04	0.17	-3.86	0.000
				Chi square	*p*
Quality of the teaching	1	0.21	0.30	15.66	0.0001
Teaching did not suit me	1	0.29	0.37	13.25	0.0003
Class size too large	1	0.15	0.20	7.66	0.0057
Organization of the programme	1	0.25	0.32	7.87	0.0050
Lack of personal support from staff	1	0.23	0.29	6.88	0.0087
Lack of study skills	2	0.15	0.22	11.08	0.0009
Programme not relevant to career	4	0.21	0.29	11.92	0.0006
Financial problems	5	0.35	0.43	10.64	0.0011
Institution not as expected	6, 1, 2	0.17	0.24	14.48	0.0001
Institutional computing provision	6	0.08	0.14	13.64	0.0002
Institutional provision of social facilities	6	0.08	0.13	11.20	0.0008
Institutional provision of specialist equipment	6	0.06	0.11	12.61	0.0004

(e)(i) Comparison by gender (full-time and sandwich students only)

Appendices

Variable	Component of factor no.	Female N=1118 Mean	Male N=1026 Mean	t / Chi square	p
Factor 1		-0.01	0.02	0.58	ns
Factor 2		0.00	0.01	0.19	ns
Factor 3		0.09	-0.10	-4.36	0.0000
Factor 4		-0.14	0.16	6.93	0.0000
Factor 5		-0.06	0.07	3.00	0.0030
Factor 6		-0.03	0.04	1.55	ns
				Chi square	*p*
Difficulty of the programme	2	0.18	0.24	14.05	0.0012
Lack of study skills	2	0.13	0.21	22.95	0.0000
Lack of personal support from students	2	0.17	0.13	7.50	0.0062
Insufficient academic progress	2	0.26	0.34	16.16	0.0000
Homesickness	3	0.14	0.07	24.85	0.0000
Programme not relevant to career	4	0.20	0.25	7.84	0.0051
Lack of commitment to programme	4	0.31	0.46	50.67	0.0000
Needed a break from education	4	0.26	0.31	8.20	0.0042
Financial problems	5	0.32	0.43	28.36	0.0000
Demands of employment whilst studying	5	0.13	0.17	8.24	0.0041
Needs of dependants	5	0.18	0.12	12.02	0.0005
Emotional difficulties with others	5	0.26	0.20	9.52	0.0020
Health problems	–	0.26	0.20	8.35	0.0039
Problems with drugs/alcohol	–	0.04	0.11	38.81	0.0000
Pregnancy/partner's pregnancy	–	0.08	0.01	12.64	0.0004

(e)(ii) Comparison by gender (part-time students only)

Variable	Female N=211 Mean	Male N=114 Mean	t	p
Factor 1	-0.04	0.08	-1.05	ns
Factor 2	-0.04	0.07	-0.94	ns
Factor 3	0.03	-0.05	0.62	ns
Factor 4	0.05	-0.10	1.26	ns
Factor 5	0.00	-0.01	0.05	ns
Factor 6	-0.01	0.03	-0.28	ns

	Component of factor no.			Chi square	p
Insufficient academic progress	1	0.05	0.12	4.26	0.0390
Difficulty of the programme	2, 1	0.06	0.17	8.06	0.0045
Needs of dependants	4	0.31	0.17	7.00	0.0082

(f) Comparison by type of institution (full-time and sandwich students only)

Variable	Component of factor no.	College N=325 Mean	Post-1992 U N=1291 Mean	Pre-1992 U N=528 Mean	F	p
Factor 1		-0.03	0.02	-0.01	0.38	ns
Factor 2		0.02	-0.06	0.16	9.12	0.0001
Factor 3		-0.08	-0.03	0.10	4.28	0.0140
Factor 4		-0.08	-0.01	0.08	2.89	ns
Factor 5		0.03	0.04	-0.09	3.36	0.0349
Factor 6		0.09	-0.01	-0.03	1.37	ns
					Chi square	p
Difficulty of the programme	2	0.19	0.19	0.26	11.37	0.0034
Difficulty in making friends	3	0.07	0.08	0.13	15.38	0.0005
Homesickness	3	0.07	0.10	0.14	11.36	0.0034
Chose wrong field of study	4	0.34	0.38	0.44	9.82	0.0074
Lack of commitment to programme	4	0.35	0.36	0.43	9.66	0.0080
Institutional library provision	6	0.15	0.07	0.07	18.39	0.0001

(g)(i) Comparison by level of programme (full-time and sandwich students only)

Variable	Sub-degree N=213 Mean	Degree N=1828 Mean	*t*	*p*
Factor 1	0.14	−0.01	−1.92	ns
Factor 2	−0.06	0.02	1.02	ns
Factor 3	−0.09	0.01	1.43	ns
Factor 4	0.02	0.00	−0.27	ns
Factor 5	0.10	−0.01	−1.43	ns
Factor 6	0.18	−0.02	−2.40	ns

	Component of factor no.	Sub-degree	Degree	*Chi square*	*p*
Programme not relevant to career	4	0.30	0.22	6.65	0.0099
Institutional computing provision	6	0.17	0.08	15.40	0.0001
Institutional provision of specialist equipment	6	0.12	0.07	7.55	0.0060

(g)(ii) Comparison by level of programme (part-time students only)

Variable	Sub-degree N=105 Mean	Degree N=207 Mean	t	p
Factor 1	0.06	−0.03	0.74	ns
Factor 2	−0.16	0.07	−1.93	ns
Factor 3	−0.04	0.02	−0.55	ns
Factor 4	−0.22	0.10	−2.94	0.004
Factor 5	−0.09	0.05	−1.12	ns
Factor 6	0.12	−0.06	1.47	ns

	Component of factor no.			Chi square	p
Demands of employment whilst studying	2	0.42	0.56	5.02	0.0251
Needs of dependants	4	0.17	0.30	5.73	0.0167
Financial problems	4	0.15	0.27	4.46	0.0346
Health problems	4	0.08	0.21	7.88	0.0050

(h) Comparison by match of entry qualifications to programme (full-time and sandwich students only)

Variable	Good N=1108 Mean	Partial N=265 Mean	Weak N=73 Mean	F	p
Factor 1	0.03	-0.09	0.00	1.57	ns
Factor 2	0.02	-0.09	-0.06	1.28	ns
Factor 3	0.09	0.05	0.04	0.19	ns
Factor 4	0.08	0.23	0.17	2.76	ns
Factor 5	-0.08	-0.07	-0.18	0.38	ns
Factor 6	-0.04	-0.04	0.14	1.14	ns
				Chi square	*p*
Chose wrong field of study *Component of factor no.* 4	0.40	0.53	0.54	17.88	0.0001

(i) Comparison by number of subjects in the programme (full-time and sandwich students only)

Variable	Single-subject N=1110 Mean	Multi-subject N=845 Mean	t	p
Factor 1	0.04	-0.06	-2.15	ns
Factor 2	0.06	-0.05	-2.35	ns
Factor 3	0.01	-0.01	-0.45	ns
Factor 4	0.03	-0.02	-1.07	ns
Factor 5	-0.03	0.03	1.39	ns
Factor 6	-0.03	0.07	2.06	ns
			Chi square	*p*
Insufficient academic progress	0.34	0.26	13.42	0.0003

Component of factor no.
2, 4, 1

(j)(i) Comparison by social class (full-time and sandwich students only)

Variable	Component of factor no.	1 Working class N=490 Mean	2 No particular class N=518 Mean	3 Middle/upper class N=576 Mean	F	p	Inter-group significant differences (Bonferroni)
Factor 1		-0.07	-0.10	0.02	1.94	ns	
Factor 2		-0.01	0.04	-0.10	2.61	ns	
Factor 3		-0.07	-0.06	0.12	5.80	0.0031	3 v. 1, 2
Factor 4		-0.15	-0.18	0.02	6.18	0.0021	3 v. 1, 2
Factor 5		0.13	0.03	-0.27	24.19	0.0000	3 v. 1, 2
Factor 6		-0.08	0.01	-0.09	1.71	ns	
					Chi square	p	
Teaching did not suit me	1	0.24	0.24	0.32	11.60	0.0030	
Dislike of city/town	3	0.13	0.11	0.20	19.65	0.0001	
Chose wrong field of study	4	0.34	0.32	0.43	15.78	0.0004	
Programme not relevant to career	4	0.16	0.16	0.23	11.61	0.0034	
Financial problems	5	0.44	0.38	0.24	49.66	0.0000	
Demands of employment whilst studying	5	0.17	0.14	0.09	12.82	0.0017	
Lack of personal support from family	5	0.14	0.14	0.09	10.74	0.0047	
Needs of dependants	5	0.19	0.18	0.11	13.46	0.0012	
Travel difficulties	5	0.19	0.15	0.11	16.32	0.0003	

(j)(ii) Comparison by social class (part-time students only)

Variable	1 Working class N=100 Mean	2 No particular class N=114 Mean	3 Middle/upper class N=104 Mean	F	p	Inter-group significant differences (Bonferroni)
Factor 1	-0.02	-0.15	0.20	3.36	0.0360	2 v. 3
Factor 2	0.05	0.03	-0.06	0.36	ns	
Factor 3	-0.06	-0.06	0.14	1.43	ns	
Factor 4	-0.13	0.16	-0.07	2.46	ns	
Factor 5	0.00	0.04	-0.03	0.15	ns	
Factor 6	-0.06	0.01	0.09	0.57	ns	

	Component of factor no.			Chi square	p	
Organization of the programme	1	0.22	0.14	0.31	8.87	0.0119
Quality of the teaching	1	0.18	0.13	0.27	6.78	0.0337

References

ABRAMSON, M. (1994) 'Franchising, access, quality and exclusivity: some observations from recent research into further and higher education partnerships', *Journal of Access Studies*, **9**, pp. 109–14.

ASTIN, A.W. (1970) 'The methodology of research on college impact (I)', *Sociology of Education*, **43**, pp. 223–54.

ASTIN, A.W. (1985) *Achieving Educational Excellence*, San Fransisco, CA: Jossey-Bass.

ASTIN, A.W. (1991) *Assessment for Excellence*, New York: American Council on Education and Macmillan.

ASTIN, A.W., TSUI, L. and AVALOS, J. (1996) *Degree Attainment Rates at American Colleges and Universities: Effects of Race, Gender and Institutional Type*, Los Angeles, CA: Higher Education Research Institute, University of California.

BEAN, J.P. (1983) 'The application of a model of turnover in work organizations to the student attrition process', *Review of Higher Education*, **6**, pp. 129–48.

BEAN, J.P. and METZNER, B.S. (1985) 'A conceptual model of nontraditional undergraduate student attrition', *Review of Educational Research*, **55**, pp. 485–540.

BENTHAM, M. (1998) 'Universities hit by a record number of drop-outs', *The Sunday Telegraph*, 9 August, p. 1.

BIRD, J., CRAWLEY, G. and SHEIBANI, A. (1993) *Franchising and Access to Higher Education: A Study of HE/FE Collaboration*, Sheffield: Department of Employment.

BLUMBERG, A.S., LAVIN, D.E., LERER, N. and KOVATH, J. (1997) *Graduation Rates and Inferences of Institutional Effectiveness*, paper presented at the Annual Forum of the Association for Institutional Research, Orlando (mimeo).

BLUNDELL, R., DEARDEN, L., GOODMAN, A. and REED, H. (1997) *Higher Education, Employment and Earnings in Britain*, London: Institute for Fiscal Studies.

BODDY, G. (1996) *A Three Year Longitudinal Study of the University Experience — A Progress Report*, paper presented at the Asia Pacific Student Services Association Conference, Sydney (mimeo).

BOURNER, T., with REYNOLDS, A., HAMED, M. and BARNETT, R. (1991) *Part-time Students and Their Experience of Higher Education*, Buckingham: SRHE and the Open University Press.

BRADY, D. and METCALFE, A. (1994) 'Staff and student perceptions of franchising', *Journal of Access Studies*, **9**, pp. 271–7.

BRAXTON, J.M., VESPER, N. and HOSSLER, D. (1995) 'Expectations for college and student persistence', *Research in Higher Education*, **36**, pp. 595–612.

CABRERA, A.F., CASTAÑEDA, M.B., NORA, A. and HENGSTLER, D. (1992) 'The convergence between two theories of college persistence', *Journal of Higher Education*, **63**, pp. 143–64.

CAVE, M., HANNEY, S., HENKEL, M. and KOGAN, M. (1997) *The Use of Performance Indicators in Higher Education*, 3rd edn, London: Jessica Kingsley.

CERI (1997) *Education Policy Analysis 1997*, Paris: Centre for Educational Research and Innovation, Organization for Economic Cooperation and Development.

CHAPMAN, K. (1994) 'Variability of degree results in geography in United Kingdom Universities, 1973–1990: preliminary results and policy implications', *Studies in Higher Education*, **19**, pp. 89–102.

CLARE, J. (1997) '100,000 student drop-outs cost £90m a year', *The Daily Telegraph*, 17 December, pp. 1–2.

CONFEDERATION OF BRITISH INDUSTRY (1994) *Thinking Ahead: Ensuring Expansion of Higher Education into the 21st Century*, London: CBI.

CVCP (1995a) *Higher Education Management Statistics: A Future Strategy*, London: Committee of Vice Chancellors and Principals.

CVCP (1995b) *Students Leaving for Non-academic Reasons Jump 30% in One Year* (press release, 28 June), London: Committee of Vice Chancellors and Principals.

DAVIES, P. (1997) *Within our control? Improving retention rates in FE*, paper presented at HEIST conferences 'Maximizing Student Retention in FHE: Current Research, Issues and Policy', Leeds and London (mimeo).

DENNIS, S. (ed.) (1998) *The PUSH Guide to Which University 99*, Maidenhead: McGraw-Hill.

DEPARTMENT OF EDUCATION AND SCIENCE (1992) *Statistical Bulletin 9/92*, London: DES.

DILLMAN, D.A. (1978) *Mail and Telephone Surveys*, New York: Wiley.

DOBSON, I., SHARMA, R. and HAYDON, A. (1996) *Evaluation of the Relative Performance of Commencing Undergraduate Students in Australian Universities*, Adelaide: Australian Credit Transfer Agency.

DOBSON, I. and SHARMA, R. (1998) Student performance and the cost of failure, paper presented at the 20th Annual EAIR Forum (9–12 September), San Sebastián, Spain, mimeo.

DUBOIS, P.H. (1963) *An Introduction to Psychological Statistics*, New York: Harper and Row.

ENTWISTLE, N. and RAMSDEN, P. (1983) *Understanding Student Learning*, London: Croom Helm.

EWELL, P.T. and JONES, D.P. (1994) 'Pointing the way: indicators as policy tools in higher education', in RUPPERT, S.S. (ed.) *Charting Higher Education Accountability: A Sourcebook on State-level Performance Indicators*, Denver, CO: Education Commission of the States, pp. 6–16.

EWELL, P., with LOVELL, C.D., DRESSLER, P. and JONES, D.P. (1993) *A Preliminary Study of the Feasibility and Utility for National Policy of the Instructional 'Good Practice' Indicators in Undergraduate Education*, Boulder, CO: National Center for Higher Education Management Systems.

FENNELL, S. (1997) 'Can the door to lifelong learning be opened by the key to completion?', unpublished report of a research project conducted by the Career Development Centre at the University of Derby.

FOLGER, J. and JONES, D.P. (1993) *Using Fiscal Policy to Achieve State Education Goals*, Denver, CO: Education Commission of the States.

GAITHER, G., NEDWEK, B. and NEAL, J.E. (1994) *Measuring Up: The Promises and Pitfalls of Performance Indicators in Higher Education* (ASHE-ERIC Report No. 5), Washington, DC: George Washington University.

HARTOG, J. (1983) 'To graduate or not: does it matter?' *Economics Letters*, **12**, pp. 193–9.

HASLAM, L. and CHAUDHRY, R. (1995) *Report on the Reasons Given by Students for Withdrawing from LJMU Award Programmes*, Liverpool: Liverpool John Moores University.

HEFCE (1995) *Average Units of Council Funding (AUCF) for the Academic Year 1994–95*, Bristol: Higher Education Funding Council for England.

HEFCE (1998) 'Circular letter 20/98' (22 July), Bristol: HEFCE.

HEQC (1995) *A Quality Assurance Framework for Guidance and Learner Support in Higher Education: The Guidelines*, London: Higher Education Quality Council.

HEQC (1996a) *Inter-institutional Variability of Degree Results: An Analysis in Selected Subjects*, London: Higher Education Quality Council.

HEQC (1996b) *Personal Tutoring and Academic Advice*, London: Higher Education Quality Council.

HEQC (1996c) *Strengthening External Examining*, London: Higher Education Quality Council.

HEQC (1997) *Graduate Standards Programme: Final Report*, 2 vols, London: Higher Education Quality Council.

HESA (1996) *Students in Higher Education Institutions 1994/5*, Cheltenham: Higher Education Statistics Agency.

HESA (1997) *Students in Higher Education Institutions 1995/6*, Cheltenham: Higher Education Statistics Agency.

HIGGINS, M.A. (1998) Personal communication.

HODGES, L. (1998) 'Unprepared and disillusioned: 60,000 student drop-outs', *The Independent* (supplement), 29 January, pp. 2–3.

HOLDEN, M. and LADBROOK, C. (1995) 'Students flee danger streets', *South Manchester Reporter*, no. 780, 21 December, p. 1.

HUMPHREY, R. and MCCARTHY, P., with POPHAM, F., CHARLES, Z., GARLAND, M., GOOCH, S., HORNSBY, K., HOUGHTON, C. and MULDOON, C. (1998) 'Stress and the contemporary student', *Higher Education Quarterly*, **52**, pp. 221–42.

JOHNES, J. (1990) 'Determinants of student wastage in higher education', *Studies in Higher Education*, **15**, pp. 87–99.

JOHNES, J. and TAYLOR, J. (1989) 'Undergraduate non-completion rates: differences between UK universities', *Higher Education*, **18**, pp. 209–15.

JOHNES, J. and TAYLOR, J. (1990a) *Performance Indicators in Higher Education*, Buckingham: SRHE and Open University Press.

JOHNES, J. and TAYLOR, J. (1990b) 'Undergraduate completion rates: a reply', *Higher Education*, **19**, pp. 385–90.

JOHNES, J. and TAYLOR, J. (1991) 'Non-completion of a degree course and its effect on the subsequent experience of non-completers in the labour market', *Studies in Higher Education*, **16**, pp. 73–81.

JOHNSON, G.M. (1996) 'Faculty differences in university attrition: a comparison of the characteristics of Arts, Education and Science students who withdrew from undergraduate programs', *Journal of Higher Education Policy and Management*, **18**, pp. 75–91.

JOHNSON, G.M. and BUCK, G.H. (1995) 'Students' personal and academic attributions of university withdrawal', *Canadian Journal of Higher Education*, **XXV**, 2, pp. 53–77.

JOHNSTON, V. (n.d.) *Why Do First Year Students Fail to Progress to Their Second Year? An Academic Staff Perspective*, Edinburgh: Department of Mathematics, Napier University (mimeo).

JOHNSTON, V. (1997) *Missing Persons: First Year Withdrawal During 1996/97*, paper produced for the Student Retention Project, Napier University, Edinburgh (mimeo).

JOHNSTON, V. and POLLOCK, A. (1998) *The Student Experience and Undergraduate Progression in the First Year: A Case Study of a Scottish New University*, paper presented at the Third UK Conference on Student Wellbeing in Higher Education, University of Glasgow (mimeo).

JPIWG (1994a) *Consultative Report*, Bristol: HEFCE (mimeo).

JPIWG (1994b) *Explanatory and Statistical Material to Accompany Consultative report*, Bristol: HEFCE (mimeo).

KELLY, L. (1996) *Implementing Astin's I–E–O Model in the Study of Student Retention: A Multivariate Time Dependent Approach* (Report 09-96), New London, CT: Center for Advanced Studies, United States Coast Guard Academy.

KEMBER, D. and HARPER, G. (1987) 'Implications of instruction arising from the relationship between approaches to studying and academic outcomes', *Instructional Science*, **16**, pp. 35–46.

KINGSTON, P. (1998) 'BA watch', *Guardian Higher*, 31 March, p. v.

LEWIN, K., HEUBLEIN, U., SOMMER, D. and CORDIER, H. (1995) 'Studienabbruch: Gründe und anschliessende Tätigkeiten: Ergebnisse einer bundesweiten Befragung im Studienjahr 1993/94', in *Kurzinformation*, no. A 1/95, Hanover: Hochschul-Informations-System.

LINKE, R. (Chair) (1991) *Performance Indicators in Higher Education* (Report of a trial evaluation study commissioned by the Commonwealth Department of Employment, Education and Training), 2 vols, Canberra: Australian Government Publishing Service.

LONG, M., CARPENTER, P. and HAYDEN, M. (1995) *Graduating from Higher Education*, Canberra: Australian Government Publishing Service.

McGIVNEY, V. (1996) *Staying or Leaving the Course*, Leicester: NIACE.

McINNIS, C. and JAMES, R., with McNAUGHT, C. (1995) *First Year on Campus: Diversity in the Initial Experiences of Australian Undergraduates*, Melbourne: Centre for the Study of Higher Education, University of Melbourne.

McKEOWN, B., MacDONNELL, A. and BOWMAN, C. (1993) 'The student point of view in attrition research', *Canadian Journal of Higher Education*, **23**, pp. 65–85.

McPHERSON, A. and PATERSON, L. (1990) 'Undergraduate completion rates: a comment', *Higher Education*, **19**, pp. 377–83.

METZNER, B.S. and BEAN, J.P. (1987) 'The estimation of a model of nontraditional undergraduate student attrition', *Research in Higher Education*, **27**, pp. 15–38.

MOORE, R. (1995) *Retention Rates Research Project: Final Report*, Sheffield: Division of Access and Guidance, Sheffield Hallam University (mimeo).

MOORTGAT, J.-L. (1996) *A Study of Dropout in European Higher Education: Case Studies of Five Countries*, Strasbourg: Council of Europe.

NAPOLI, A.R. and WORTMAN, P.M. (1997) *Psychosocial Factors Related to Retention and Early Departure of Two-year Community College Students*, paper presented at the Forum of the Association for Institutional Research, Orlando (mimeo).

NATWEST (1998) *One in Three Students Say Their Finances Are Out of Control* (news release 119/98), London: NatWest.

NCIHE (1997) *Higher Education in the Learning Society* (Report of the National Committee of Inquiry into Higher Education), London: HMSO.

NORUSIS, M.J. (1994) *SPSS for Windows Professional Statistics 6.1*, Chicago, IL: SPSS Inc.

NUS (1995) *Values for Money Survey: Student Finance for the Academic Year 1994/95*, London: National Union of Students.

OAKEY, D.H. and RAE, J.M. (1994) *Student Non-completion and the Management of Transition into Higher Education*, paper presented at the SRHE Conference, University of York (mimeo).

OZGA, J. and SUKHNANDAN, L. (1997) 'Undergraduate non-completion', Report No. 2 in *Undergraduate Non-completion in Higher Education in England*, Bristol: HEFCE.

OZGA, J. and SUKHNANDAN, L. (1998) 'Undergraduate non-completion: developing an explanatory model', *Higher Education Quarterly*, **52**, pp. 316–33.

PASCARELLA, E. (1985) 'College environmental influences on learning and cognitive development: a critical view and synthesis', in SMART, J. (ed.) *Higher Education: Handbook of Theory and Research*, vol. 1, New York: Agathon, pp. 1–61.

PASCARELLA, E.T. and TERENZINI, P.T. (1991) *How College Affects Students*, San Francisco, CA: Jossey-Bass.

Percy-Smith, J. and Stronach, J. (1992) *Students Withdrawing from Leeds Polytechnic Courses*, Leeds: Leeds Polytechnic (mimeo).

Postle, G.D., Clarke, J.R., Skuja, E., Bull, D.D., Batorowicz, K. and McCann, H.A. (n.d.) *Towards Excellence in Diversity: Educational Equity in the Australian Higher Education Sector in 1995. Status, Trends and Future Directions*, Toowoomba, Queensland: USQ Press.

QAA (1998) 'Consultation: developing the quality and standards assurance framework for UK higher education', *Higher Quality* (Bulletin of the Quality Assurance Agency for Higher Education), **1**, 3, March, pp. 3–23.

Ramsden, P. (1992) *Learning to Teach in Higher Education*, London: Routledge.

Richardson, J. (1995) 'Mature students in higher education: II. An investigation of approaches to studying and academic performance', *Studies in Higher Education*, **20**, pp. 5–17.

Rickinson, B. (1997) 'The relationship between undergraduate student counselling and successful degree completion', *Studies in Higher Education*, **23**, pp. 95–102.

Rickinson, B. and Rutherford, D. (1996) 'Systematic monitoring of the adjustment to university of undergraduates: a strategy for reducing withdrawal rates', *British Journal of Guidance and Counselling*, **24**, pp. 213–25.

Rickwood, P.W., Goodwin, V. and Williams, S. (1995) *Getting More: Keeping More? A Consideration of Mature Part-time Student Non-completion, Including a Comparative Study Carried Out in the West Midland Region of the Open University* (publication details not given on original).

Roberts, D. and Allen, A. (1996) *Year 12 Students' Perceptions of Higher Education*, Leeds: HEIST.

Robertson, D. (1994) *Choosing to Change; Extending Access, Choice and Mobility in Higher Education* (Report of the CAT Development Project), London: Higher Education Quality Council.

Robertson, D. (1996) *The Learning Bank and Individual Accounts — Emerging Policies for the Funding of Relationships in the Tertiary Learning Market*, paper presented at the CVCP/SRHE Research Seminar 'Paying for Higher Education: The Options', 7 November (mimeo).

Robertson, D. and Hillman, J. (1997) *Widening Participation in Higher Education for Students from Lower Socio-economic Groups and Students with Disabilities* (Report No. 6 prepared for the National Committee of Inquiry into Higher Education), London: HMSO.

Scott, P. (1995) *The Meanings of Mass Higher Education*, Buckingham: SRHE and Open University Press.

Seymour, E. and Hewitt, N.M. (1997) *Talking about Leaving: Why Undergraduates Leave the Sciences*, Oxford: Westview Press.

SHEFC (1997) *Identification of Unacceptably High Rates of Non-progression* (circular letter 34/97, 20 October), Edinburgh: SHEFC.

Shelter (1997) 'NOP Survey for Shelter/Midland Bank', London: Shelter (unpublished).

SIEGEL, S. and CASTELLAN, N.J. (1988) *Nonparametric Statistics for the Behavioral Sciences*, 2nd edn, New York: McGraw-Hill.

SILVER, H., STENNETT, A. and WILLIAMS, R. (1995) *The External Examiner System: Possible Futures* (Report of a project commissioned by the Higher Education Quality Council), London: Quality Support Centre of the Open University.

SKUJA, E. (n.d.) 'Performance of the Australian university sector in access and equity', in POSTLE, G.D. et al., op. cit., pp. 59–92.

SMITH, D., BOCOCK, J. and SCOTT, P. (1996) *Standard Systems, Non-standard Students: Experiences of Progression from Further to Higher Education*, Leeds: Centre for Policy Studies in Education, University of Leeds.

SPSS (1993) *Base System Syntax Reference Guide 6.0*, Chicago, IL: SPSS Inc.

STOWELL, M. (1998) 'Student Retention in Year 1 of the Combined Honours Degree Programme', unpublished internal report, 29 April, Nene University College, Northampton.

SUDMAN, S. and BRADBURN, N.M. (1974) *Response Effects in Surveys: A Review and Synthesis*, Chicago: Aldine.

SWAIN, H. (1998) 'Fury over flunk figures', *Times Higher Education Supplement*, no. 1345, 14 August, p. 3.

SZULECKA, T.K., SPRINGETT, N.R. and DE PAUW, K.W. (1987) 'General health, psychiatric vulnerability and withdrawal from university in first-year undergraduates', *British Journal of Guidance and Counselling*, **15**, pp. 82–91.

THOMAS, M., ADAMS, S. and BIRCHENOUGH, A. (1996) 'Student withdrawal from higher education', *Educational Management and Administration*, **24**, pp. 207–21.

TINTO, V. (1993) *Leaving College: Rethinking the Causes and Cures of Student Attrition*, 2nd edn, Chicago: University of Chicago Press.

TINTO, V. (1997) 'Classrooms as communities: exploring the educational character of student persistence', *Journal of Higher Education*, **68**, pp. 599–623.

VOLKWEIN, J.F. and LORANG, W.G. (1996) 'Characteristics of extenders: full-time students who take light credit loads and graduate in more than four years', *Research in Higher Education*, **37**, pp. 43–68.

WEIDMAN, J. (1989) 'Undergraduate socialization: a conceptual approach', in SMART, J. (ed.) *Higher Education: Handbook of Theory and Research*, vol. 5, New York: Agathon, pp. 289–322.

WOJTAS, O. (1998) 'Advice could halt quitters', *Times Higher Education Supplement*, no. 1348, 4 September, p. 3.

WOODLEY, A., WAGNER, L., SLOWEY, M., HAMILTON, M. and FULTON, O. (1987) *Choosing to Learn: Adults in Education*, Milton Keynes: Open University Press.

WRIGHTSON, J. (1996) 'Assessment performances: not just indicators but stimuli for the appraisal of assessment practice', in YORKE, M. *Indicators of Programme Quality*, London: Higher Education Quality Council, pp. 178–95.

YORKE, M. (1996a) *The Assessment of Transferable Skills in Higher Education: Towards Systemic Implementation*, Liverpool: Centre for Higher Education Development, Liverpool John Moores University.

YORKE, M. (1996b) *Indicators of Programme Quality*, London: Higher Education Quality Council.

YORKE, M. (1996c) 'The use of funding to encourage quality in academic programmes: some lessons from experience, and their applicability', *Quality in Higher Education*, **2**, pp. 33–44.

YORKE, M. (1997a) 'A good league table guide?', *Quality Assurance in Education*, **5**, pp. 61–72.

YORKE, M. (1997b) 'This way QA?', *Quality Assurance in Education*, **5**, pp. 97–100.

YORKE, M. (1998a) 'Performance indicators relating to student development: can they be trusted?', *Quality in Higher Education*, **4**, pp. 45–61.

YORKE, M. (1998b) 'The Times' "league table" of universities 1997: a statistical appraisal', *Quality Assurance in Education*, **6**, pp. 58–60.

YORKE, M., with BELL, R., DOVE, A., HASLAM, L., HUGHES JONES, H., LONGDEN, B., O'CONNELL, C., TYPUSZAK, R. and WARD, J. (1997a) 'Undergraduate non-completion in England', Report No. 1 in *Undergraduate Non-completion in Higher Education in England*, Bristol: HEFCE.

YORKE, M., with BELL, R., DOVE, A., HASLAM, L., HUGHES JONES, H., LONGDEN, B., O'CONNELL, C., TYPUSZAK, R. and WARD, J. (1997b) *Undergraduate Non-completion in England* (Extended Final Report of a research project commissioned by HEFCE), Bristol: HEFCE.

YORKE, M., MCCORMICK, D. and CHAPMAN, T. (1996) *HE 2005+: Towards a Sectoral Strategy for Teaching and Learning in Higher Education Institutions*, Bristol: HEFCE.

YOUNGMAN, M.B. (1976) *Analysing Social and Educational Research Data*, London: McGraw-Hill.

Index